THE SUNDAY LECTIONARY
RITUAL WORD, PASCHAL SHAPE

Normand Bonneau, O.M.I.

A Liturgical Press Book

THE LITURGICAL PRESS
Collegeville, Minnesota

Cover design by Ann Blattner. Illustration from *The Book of Lindisfarne,* "Carpet Page with Scattered Panels," c. 698 A.D.

Excerpts from the *Lectionary, Sundays and Solemnities,* Copyright © Concacan Inc., 1992. All rights reserved. Used by permission of the Canadian Conference of Catholic Bishops, Ottawa.

The Scripture quotations contained herein are adapted from the New Revised Standard Version of the Bible, copyrighted, 1989 by the Division of Christian Education of the National Council of the Churches of Christ in the United States of America, and are used by permission. All rights reserved.

The texts of the Vatican II documents are from Norman P. Tanner, ed., *Decrees of the Ecumenical Councils. Vol. 2: Trent to Vatican II* (London: Sheed & Ward/Washington, D.C.: Georgetown University Press, 1990). Used with permission.

1	2	3	4	5	6	7	8

Library of Congress Cataloging-in-Publication Data

Bonneau, Normand, 1948–
    The Sunday lectionary: ritual word, Paschal shape / Normand Bonneau.
        p.   cm.
    Includes bibliographical references and index.
    ISBN 0-8146-2457-X (alk. paper)
    1. Lectionaries.   2. Catholic Church—Liturgy.   I. Title.
BX2003.B58   1998
264'.02034—dc21   97–27349
                                                                CIP

For my parents
on their fiftieth anniversary
(August 5, 1996)

Contents

Abbreviations

DV	*Dei Verbum*, the Dogmatic Constitution on Divine Revelation
GNLYC	*General Norms for the Liturgical Year and the Calendar*
ICEL	*International Committee on English in the Liturgy*
ILM	Introduction to the *Lectionary for Mass* (1981 edition)
MR 1570	*Missale Romanum* (the Roman Missal) of 1570
SC	*Sacrosanctum Concilium*, the Constitution on the Sacred Liturgy

Introduction

Scripture's home is the liturgy, for in liturgical proclamation scripture becomes fully what it is, the living Word of God present and active in our midst. This is what the Vatican II documents intimate when they declare: "Christ is present through his word, in that he himself is speaking when scripture is read in church" (*SC*, no. 7); "The church has always held the divine scriptures in reverence no less than it accords to the Lord's body itself, never ceasing—*especially in the sacred liturgy*—to receive the bread of life from the one table of God's word and Christ's body, and to offer it to the faithful" (*DV*, no. 21, emphasis added). Liturgical proclamation breathes life into the dry bones of ancient inscribed words, awakening them to become the transforming, nourishing presence of the risen Christ in the world.

These rather weighty words contain the seeds of what has yet to emerge—a full-fledged theology of proclamation that would probe the significance of the public reading of scripture in the context of worship. Whatever such an endeavor might discover, surely it could not long proceed without an examination of the Lectionary, an essential, if unassuming, liturgical article without which words would not become Word. Although the revised *Ordo Lectionum Missae*—to use the official Latin title for the *Lectionary for Mass*—has been an integral part of Catholic worship since its promulgation in 1969, its history, purpose, and structure nevertheless remain relatively unknown.

This book aims to make a modest contribution to a theology of proclamation by presenting a descriptive analysis of the Sunday and Feast Day Lectionary. It is not another commentary on the readings the Lectionary contains; dozens of excellent works already render that service. Rather, this book examines the less conspicuous aspects of the Sunday Lectionary: the history of its recent reform, the principles of reading selection and distribution that inform it, and the patterns by which it shapes and structures the seasons that make up the liturgical year. Since my purpose is primarily descriptive, I have for the most part refrained from commenting on issues being discussed in current literature. It is my hope nevertheless that the information offered here will not only enrich the conversation but will also foster a deeper appreciation of the Lectionary, and through the Lectionary, of the liturgy.

My interest in the Sunday Lectionary was first kindled over a decade ago through an invitation from the editors of *Celebrate!*, a bi-monthly liturgical journal published by Novalis at Saint Paul University, Ottawa, to write short commentaries on Sunday and Feast Day Lectionary readings. In addition to these short pieces, I occasionally contributed more extensive articles in which I explored broader Lectionary issues, as, for example, the use of the Acts of the Apostles during the Easter season, or the link, on the Third, Fourth, and Fifth Sundays of Lent in Year A, between John 4, 9, and 11 and the scrutinies of the *Rite of Christian Initiation of Adults (RCIA)*. In researching the whys and wherefores of such questions, I came to realize that the Lectionary is not a random collection of biblical passages; there are reasons for the selection of readings and for the patterns in which they are arranged. Together the selection and distribution of readings form what I call the Lectionary's architecture, a design sketched in line with time-honored liturgical tradition. (Although the Lectionary also includes responsorial psalms and gospel acclamations, for the sake of keeping this study within reasonable bounds I have confined the analysis to the three biblical passages per celebration that are proclaimed, and not the two that are sung as responses).

The book gathers the results of my voyages of discovery to date. It is divided into two parts. The first, attending to more preliminary matters, surveys the history of lectionaries (chapter 1), chronicles the highlights of the Vatican II Lectionary reform (chapter 2), and examines the characteristic traits of the revised Sunday and Feast Day Lectionary (chapter 3). The second part analyzes the Lectionary's architecture for each of the liturgical seasons in turn (chapters 4 through 9). Although the chapters in Part Two can be read with profit independently of Part One, the historical background sketched in the first three chapters supplies the larger context within which to understand the Lectionary's workings in the compass of a particular season.

Most of the information found in these pages is not new. Hundreds of items pertaining more or less directly to the various aspects of the Lectionary can be found widely scattered both in learned books and periodicals as well as in more popular journals. I here present my synthesis of much of this material. To make the information accessible to as broad a readership as possible, I have kept footnotes and other scholarly apparatus to a bare minimum. I must nevertheless express my indebtedness to one study without which I would never have ventured to write a book on the Lectionary, the magisterial and comprehensive German tome by Elmar Nübold entitled *Entstehung und Bewertung der neuen Perikopenordnung des Römischen Ritus für die Messfeier an Sonn- und Festtagen* (Paderborn: Verlag Bonifatius-Druckerei, 1986) [*Formation and Appraisal of the Roman Rite's New Order of Readings for the Celebration of Mass on Sundays and Solemnities*]. I have indicated in the notes where I have drawn directly from it, but its influence can be felt throughout. As vast and as important as the secondary literature on the Lectionary is, however, it does not exempt one from reading the Lectionary itself (the edition consulted here is the *LECTIONARY: Sundays and Solemnities,* published by the Canadian Conference of Catholic Bishops, Ottawa, 1992, and uses the *NRSV*) and the official documents pertaining to it. In particular, anyone wishing to understand the Lectionary and how it works must be conversant with Vatican II's Constitution on the Sacred Liturgy (*Sacrosanctum Concilium*) and Dogmatic Constitution on Divine Revelation (*Dei Verbum*), as well as with the ancillary documents the *General Norms for the Liturgical Year and the Calendar* and the Introduction to the *Lectionary for Mass* (especially the 1981 revision of the original 1969 edition). These documents are simply indispensable, and I quote freely from them throughout the book. I can only urge that they be consulted firsthand and in their entirety.

Finally, I wish to thank the many friends and colleagues whose interest in and encouragement of this project have never flagged, particularly those who (they know who they are) took upon themselves the unenviable task of nagging me about it until I should bring it to completion. In particular, I owe a special debt of gratitude to Bernadette Gasslein who kindly accepted to edit the manuscript. Her liturgical insight and grammatical acumen have been invaluable. I am pleased to acknowledge that this book was subsidized in part by a grant from Saint Paul University.

Ottawa, Feast of St. Jerome, 1996

PART ONE

HISTORY OF THE LECTIONARY AND ITS REFORM

1   A Brief History of Lectionaries

"Without a doubt, the massive introduction of Scripture in the missal constitutes the most spectacular renewal of the Council's liturgical reform."[1] In these words Adrien Nocent, one of the members of the Vatican II committee for the revision of the Lectionary, evaluates the significance of the achievement. Never before in the history of liturgy had such a thorough and informed revision of the Lectionary been done.

Vatican II sought to reform the liturgy, not create it anew, for liturgy, as the living tradition of the Church, demands continuity. At every stage of their work, the redactors of the revised Lectionary returned to tradition, particularly tradition hallowed by time-tested practice. This was to assure that the adaptation of the Lectionary for the modern world remained solidly anchored in the centuries-long experience of countless Christian communities.

To understand and appreciate the revised Lectionary, then, it is important to place the Vatican II reform in the larger context of the history of lectionaries. This chapter offers a rapid historical survey of the Jewish and Christian traditions that underlie the *Ordo Lectionum Missae*. A definition of lectionary sets the stage for what follows.

What Is a Lectionary?

A lectionary is an "orderly sequence of selections from Scripture to be read aloud at public worship by a religious community."[2] This definition contains three important elements. First, a lectionary is not the Bible

---

[1] Adrien Nocent, "La parole de Dieu et Vatican II," in Pierre Jounel, Reiner Kaczynski, Gottardo Pasqualette, eds., *Liturgia, opera divina e umana: studi sulla riforma liturgica offerti a S. E. Mons. Annibale Bugnini in occasione del suo 70ᵉ compleano* (Roma: Edizioni liturgiche, 1982) 136 (my translation).

[2] John Reumann, "A History of Lectionaries: From the Synagogue at Nazareth to Post-Vatican II," *Interpretation* 31 (1977) 116.

as such, but passages selected from the Bible. It is a product of one of the many ways a community appropriates the Bible for the purposes of worship. Second, the passages are not presented in a helter-skelter fashion but are selected and organized in patterns according to specific principles. Third, since the selected and ordered passages from scripture are to be used at public worship, the type and frequency of a community's public worship will greatly determine how passages are chosen and distributed. These three aspects of a lectionary are always present and always mutually influencing each other; a difference in one aspect (different selections, or different principles, or different kinds of worship) influences the configuration of the whole.

Since Vatican II, the word "lectionary" evokes in the mind of Roman Catholics a large, ornate, and imposing book containing the scriptural passages proclaimed at the Eucharist. The *Lectionary for Mass* is in fact a collection of *six* different Lectionaries, all sharing the common feature of containing biblical passages selected to be read at eucharistic celebrations.[3] Printed in one book or in several volumes, the *Lectionary for Mass* comprises a Lectionary for Sundays and Solemnities (solemnities here means feasts of the Lord which do not usually occur or never fall on a Sunday, such as Christmas, Epiphany, the Easter Triduum, Ascension), a Lectionary for weekday Masses, a Lectionary for Masses on saints' days, a Lectionary for ritual Masses (confirmation, marriage, funerals, etc.), a Lectionary for Masses for various occasions (for the Church, for civil needs, etc.), and a Lectionary for votive Masses.

The Lectionary for Sundays and Solemnities, the subject of this study, is the most important of the several Lectionaries for Mass, for it is on Sundays and Solemnities that Christians traditionally gather to celebrate the Lord's resurrection. As the following chapters will show, that this Lectionary is read at the Sunday Eucharist totally influences the selection and distribution of the biblical passages it contains.

A Brief History of Lectionaries

The Vatican II revision of the Lectionary, like the entire reform of the liturgy, sought to return to the sources of Christian practice and experi-

---

[3]The *Lectionary for Mass* is one of two kinds of Lectionaries used by Roman Catholics. The other type of Lectionary is designed for the Liturgy of the Hours (formerly known as the "breviary"). Consisting primarily of psalms and intercessions, the Liturgy of the Hours also has embedded in it a selection of scriptural readings.

ence. But since all things Christian rest on the foundation of Jewish traditions, a history of lectionaries necessarily begins with the people of Israel. In fact, many of the patterns underlying the newly revised Roman Catholic Sunday Lectionary replicate those of the ancient Jewish lectionaries.

Jewish Lectionary Tradition

Before Christians arrived on the stage of history, Jewish communities had already developed an extensive order of scriptural passages designed to be read at their weekly Sabbath synagogue services. Synagogue is a Greek word meaning "assembly, gathering"; by extension it also came to mean the room or building where people assembled. Although archaeological evidence of synagogue buildings reaches back only to the second century before Christ, many scholars believe that the Jewish tradition of assembling regularly for prayer and for the study of the scriptures dates back to the time of the Babylonian Exile (587–535 B.C.). These years marked a traumatic period for the Jewish people. Invaded, conquered, and subjugated by the Babylonians, those who escaped slaughter fled to neighboring lands while the elite were carried off into exile. Judah and its capital city Jerusalem were laid waste. The people had lost their homeland, their monarchy and, most importantly, their temple in Jerusalem. Without a temple they could not offer animal sacrifices, their principal form of worship. The only rallying point for worship among the deported Jews in Babylon or among the refugees in the *diaspora* (Greek for "dispersion") were the scriptures. It was probably in these circumstances that the Jewish people developed what could be called a "Liturgy of the Word" for which they regularly gathered on the Sabbath.

Once the Exile was over, many Jews returned from Babylon to their homeland. They reconstructed the temple in Jerusalem and reinstituted animal sacrifices. However, even with this restoration, the tradition of the "Liturgy of the Word" in synagogue continued to spread and develop. Not only did the Jews who had remained in their adoptive lands continue to gather in synagogue, but even those in Judah and Jerusalem, who had easy access to the temple, did so as well. Meeting in synagogue became one of the distinctive traits of Jewish people everywhere. By the time of Jesus, the practice was already considered an ancient tradition, and a synagogue building was a standard feature in most Jewish communities both in Palestine and in the *diaspora*. The institution of the synagogue allowed Judaism to survive the second destruction of the temple by the Romans in A.D. 70. Without the synagogue, there might very well be no Judaism today.

Scripture in the Ancient Synagogue

There is unambiguous information about how the scriptures were read in synagogues in the sixth century after Christ.[4] The high point of the synagogue Sabbath service was the reading of an excerpt from the Torah, the first five books of the Bible (Genesis, Exodus, Leviticus, Numbers, and Deuteronomy) that Jews hold especially sacred. The Babylonian tradition divided the entire Torah into fifty-four sequential segments that were read over a one-year cycle of Sabbaths. The Palestinian tradition read the Torah in 154 sequential segments extended over a three-year cycle of Sabbaths. The Babylonian tradition's one-year cycle, which prevailed, is the one used in synagogues today. (The revised Sunday Lectionary's counterpart to the Torah reading is a passage from one of the four gospels, read last rather than first. Also, the principle of sequential reading of biblical books, slightly altered in the form of semicontinuous reading, is a key feature of the Sundays in Ordinary Time of the current Lectionary.)

In addition to the first reading from the Torah, each Sabbath synagogue service also included a second reading selected from what the Jewish tradition identifies as the Prophets (Joshua, Judges, 1 and 2 Samuel, 1 and 2 Kings constituted the "former prophets"; Isaiah, Jeremiah, Ezekiel, and the twelve minor prophets constituted the "latter prophets"). Called the *haftorah* (Aramaic for "dismissal"), this prophetic passage explained, amplified, or otherwise complemented the theme of the Torah excerpt of the day. (The pairing of two passages from different sections of the scriptures is also a feature of the revised Sunday Lectionary, where in most instances the Old Testament reading is selected in function of the gospel passage of the day.)

Every year, the calendar feasts of Passover, Pentecost, and Tabernacles interrupted the sequence of Torah readings. Even if these feasts did not fall on the Sabbath, they nevertheless required the reading, at least on contiguous Sabbaths, of passages consonant with the event the feasts celebrated. In these cases the normally prescribed sequential excerpt from the Torah, with its accompanying *haftorah*, was set aside. The major liturgical feasts, then, recurring in a *yearly* cycle, interrupted the *weekly* cycle of sabbaths. (Similarly in the Christian liturgical year the festal seasons of

---

[4]The following information on scripture in the synagogue is drawn in great part from Charles Perrot, "The Reading of the Bible in the Ancient Synagogue," *Mikra: Text, Translation, Reading, and Interpretation of the Hebrew Bible in Ancient Judaism and Early Christianity*, ed. Martin Jan Mulder (Philadelphia: Fortress, 1988) 137–59.

Advent-Christmas and Lent-Easter interrupt the semicontinuous weekly sequence of readings in Ordinary Time.)

If, then, a lectionary is "an orderly sequence of selections from Scripture to be read aloud at public worship," by the sixth century A.D. the Jewish tradition of lectionaries exhibited the following features: a sequential reading from the Torah, paired with a *haftorah* from the prophets, interrupted by special readings at the annual high feasts, proclaimed at the weekly Sabbath synagogue service.[5]

But what did the synagogue service of readings entail six centuries earlier at the time of the New Testament? Here, clear information is more difficult to come by. Most probably the fundamental features of the later, fully elaborated service were already in place. Ample evidence dating from a century or more before Jesus attests to a regular system of readings, especially of the Torah. Indeed, some Jews of that era already considered the reading of the Torah on the Sabbath a tradition so ancient that it had been inaugurated by Moses! No precise information exists, however, as to how the readings were selected and distributed. In any event, Sabbath and scripture were intimately joined: "The Bible can be read apart from a sabbath meeting, but is a sabbath meeting thinkable without such reading, which really makes it what it is?"[6] By the first century A.D. the tradition of regular Sabbath readings was widespread and firmly established, as a telling comment in James' speech in Acts of the Apostles indicates: "For in every city, for generations past, Moses has had those who proclaim him, for he has been read aloud every sabbath in the synagogues" (15:21). Chances are that the incident of Jesus reading an excerpt from the prophet Isaiah in the synagogue at Nazareth (Luke 4:15-21) points to a system of *haftorah* readings as well.

The Bible itself provides evidence for the practice of selecting special readings for major occasions. For example, Deuteronomy 31:9-11, Nehemiah 8:18, and 2 Kings 23:1-3 indicate that certain texts were read on important celebrations at the temple in Jerusalem. Although these instances do not specify the Sabbath, that the Bible gives warrant for such a practice suggests that at the time of Jesus it must have been implemented even for the Sabbaths surrounding the high liturgical feasts. It comes as no

[5]In addition, the full synagogue service also included opening blessings before the first reading, a psalm sung between the two readings, a homily following the second reading, and final prayers and blessings. Most of the elements of the synagogue service of late antiquity, then, have their counterparts in today's Roman Catholic Liturgy of the Word. Patterns of worship hallowed by tried and true tradition remain perennially valid.

[6]Charles Perrot, "The Reading of the Bible in the Ancient Synagogue," 150.

surprise, then, that such tried-and-true principles of reading selection and reading distribution—a sequential reading on a weekly cycle, interrupted by specially selected readings for the yearly feasts, and the pairing of readings from different categories of scripture according to themes—inspired the revision of the Sunday Lectionary.

Early Christian Worship

Since the first Christians in Jerusalem were Jews by birth, they continued to worship both at the temple and at the synagogue. In addition, however, Christians had their own special assemblies at which they broke the bread in commemoration of Jesus. There is no evidence of the role scripture played in these gatherings (see Acts 1–5), nor that Christians took over the lectionary system of the synagogue.

The New Testament texts themselves contain attestations of the early Christian use of the scriptures (here, of course, meaning the Old Testament) for worship. Examples appear in such exhortations as: "Do not get drunk with wine, for that is debauchery; but be filled with the Spirit, as you sing psalms and hymns and spiritual songs among yourselves, singing and making melody to the Lord in your hearts, giving thanks to God the Father at all times and for everything in the name of our Lord Jesus Christ" (Eph 5:18-20); "Let the word of Christ dwell in you richly; teach and admonish one another in all wisdom; and with gratitude in your hearts sing psalms, hymns, and spiritual songs to God" (Col 3:16); "Until I arrive, give attention to the public reading of scripture, to exhorting, to teaching" [the words "of scripture" not in the Greek text] (1 Tim 4:13). None of these cases mentions a Sunday eucharistic setting.

Although not yet considered scripture, the letters of Paul were read aloud to the community—perhaps the community assembled for worship: "I solemnly command you by the Lord that this letter be read to all [the brothers and sisters]" (1 Thess 5:27). In imitation of Paul, the author of the Letter to the Colossians does the same, yet adds injunctions about another letter that no one has yet found: "And when this letter has been read among you, have it read also in the church of the Laodiceans; and see that you read also the letter from Laodicia" (Col 4:16). In addition to these exhortations to pray the scriptures and to read the letters aloud to the assembled community, the many hymns, fragments of hymns, and canticles in the New Testament, all of them very much inspired by the scriptures, point to an early Christian appropriation of the scriptures for worship.[7]

---

[7]For example, John 1:1-18; Phil 2:5-11; Col 1:15-20; Eph 1:3-14; 1 Tim 3:15; 2 Tim 2:11-13; Luke 1:46-55; 1:68-79; 2:29-32.

Thus, even if no direct evidence of the patterned use of scripture readings in the first decades of the Church exists, the New Testament books strongly suggest that the earliest communities enjoyed a rich liturgical life in which the scriptures played a major role. Indeed, some scholars maintain that the liturgical matrix of the early churches is the most probable setting for the emergence of the New Testament texts themselves. They detect liturgical influence in the formulation and structure of such New Testament passages as the baptism of Jesus, the narrative of the Last Supper, as well as the entire Book of Revelation.

Scripture and the Sunday Eucharist

Sunday was the original Christian feast, the day of the week when Christians gathered to celebrate the Eucharist in commemoration of Jesus' resurrection. Although already the New Testament indicates that Christians regularly met on the Lord's day, nothing in the texts themselves sheds light on the way scripture was used, if it was used at all, at these services.

According to Paul's First Letter to the Corinthians, the Christians at Corinth celebrated the Eucharist in the context of a regular meal (11:17-22). If the words of the narrative in Luke 22:20 are interpreted at face value ("And he did the same with the cup *after supper*"), it would also appear that a meal, in this instance the annual Passover meal, separated the blessing over the bread and the blessing over the wine at Jesus' last supper. Soon after the time of Paul the intervening meal was discontinued—perhaps due to problems this practice engendered—and the two blessings over the bread and over the wine brought together. Did Christians read scripture at the earliest Eucharists, which included a meal? Or did they add scripture readings to their eucharistic celebration later in the first century, after the accompanying meal was dropped? Sources remain surprisingly silent on this point.

Justin Martyr provides the first unambiguous attestation, dated around A.D. 150, of Christians reading scripture at the Sunday eucharistic celebration:

> On the day which is dedicated to the sun, all those who live in the cities and who dwell in the countryside gather in a common meeting, and for as long as there is time the Memoirs of the Apostles or the writings of the prophets are read. Then, when the reader has finished, the president verbally gives a warning and appeal for the imitation of these good examples. Then we all rise together and offer prayers, and, as we said before, when our prayer is ended, bread is brought forward along with

wine and water, and the president likewise gives thanks to the best of his
ability, and the people call out their assent, saying the *Amen*. Then there
is the distribution to each and the participation in the Eucharistic elements, which also are sent with the deacons to those who are absent
(*First Apology*, 67).[8]

There are three things worth noting in Justin's description. First, by the
term "Memoirs of the Apostles" Justin most probably means the gospels,
while the word "prophets" probably includes the entire Old Testament. If
this is so, then, although as yet there is no formal collection of books called
the "New Testament," Christians considered some of their writings special
enough to be paired with scripture and read aloud at a worship service.
Second, Justin's comment that the readings went "for as long as there is
time" unfortunately gives no indication of any particular order of reading
distribution, whether sequential reading or special selections. If any pattern
existed at this early stage of the liturgy, it would probably have been some
form of sequential reading. Third, there is no indication of an annual celebration of feasts. The weekly celebration remains the only explicitly mentioned pattern of worship—a Sunday Eucharist at which scripture is read.

Nevertheless, this early practice of Christians contains the kernel of
later developments. First, the reading of the gospels at the Sunday
Eucharist was to become the one most consistent practice of all the later
Churches. It almost goes without saying that the Eucharist, which celebrates the death and resurrection of the Lord, would call forth stories
about him. Second, the reading of the Old Testament at the Sunday eucharistic celebration points to one of the key characteristics of most
Christian Lectionaries, including the newly revised Sunday Lectionary:
the Old Testament is interpreted in the light of Christ. In the words of one
author, ". . . it is unthinkable that such a reading [from the Old
Testament] in a service led by Christians would have been left without an
interpretation relating it to Christ."[9] The power of Sunday as the day commemorating the resurrection of Jesus, plus the celebration of the
Eucharist, centered as it is on the paschal mystery of Jesus, conspire to
make such an outcome inevitable. Indeed, the New Testament itself provides the warrant for this practice, for it consistently reads the scriptures
in light of the Christ event. The Sunday Lectionary, then, continues the
ancient trajectory launched by the New Testament.

[8]Quoted from W. A. Jurgens, *The Faith of the Early Fathers*, vol. 1 (Collegeville: The
Liturgical Press, 1970) 55–6.
[9]Klaus-Peter Jörns, "Liturgy: Cradle of Scripture?" *Studia Liturgica* 22 (1992) 21.

Third, the readings come before the eucharistic meal and not after. Perhaps this was done in order to allow the catechumens to participate in the liturgy as much as possible. Since they were not yet baptized, catechumens could not attend, let alone participate in, the Eucharist; however, they were allowed to hear the word of God and to learn from the readings and the homily. At least this is the reason given for the practice early in the next century by Hippolytus in his *Apostolic Tradition* (c. 215). But there is also a ritual logic in placing the readings first. In this way they announce what the Eucharist means and how the paschal mystery it celebrates is the fulfillment of salvation history. In addition, the placement of the readings stands as a reminder that it is God's word that gathers the Church, for the community assembled for prayer finds its identity and its *raison d'être* in the story of salvation proclaimed.

The Earliest Christian Lectionaries

That a lectionary is an orderly sequence of selections from scripture for use at a religious community's public worship implies principles of selection, and principles of selection in turn depend upon the kind of worship and its frequency. If, as was probably the case, the early use of scripture at the Sunday Eucharist was in the form of sequential reading, there was no need for a lectionary containing a prescribed order of biblical passages. The advent of annual feasts and seasons, however, added a new dimension to Christian worship. Special times and seasons require specially selected biblical books and passages. Until they had begun to develop a liturgical year, therefore, Christians felt no need for a lectionary.

The first hints of a liturgical year begin to appear in the second century with the emergence of an annual commemoration of the death and resurrection of the Lord at Passover time. By the third century, there is evidence that Christians had begun reading certain scriptural books, or selections from books, to celebrate Easter. The following words from William Skudlarek explain the link between the liturgical year and the Lectionary: "And when lectionaries do begin to make their appearance (or, if not lectionaries, then at least evidence for the practice of reading certain parts of the Bible at certain times of the year: Acts before Pentecost, Acts and Revelation between Easter and Pentecost, Genesis during Lent, Job and John in Passion Week), that appearance was due to the development of the liturgical year."[10]

___

[10]William Skudlarek, *The Word in Worship: Preaching in a Liturgical Context* (Nashville: Abingdon, 1981) 19.

In the fourth century, after Constantine became emperor of the Roman Empire in 312, the liturgy flourished as never before. The year after his accession to the throne, Constantine decreed the Christian faith a licit religion, and with the stroke of a pen ended the age of persecution. By the end of the century one of his successors proclaimed Christianity the only licit religion of the empire. Now officially established, the Church enjoyed the freedom to expand and grow without opposition. In order to fulfill its role as the religion of the empire, Christianity took on many of the trappings of the imperial court. This was reflected in the liturgy by more imposing and solemn ritual, large and well-ordered assemblies that gathered in basilicas, and a more complete and elaborate liturgical year. The seasons of Lent and Easter were expanded and enriched, and the first elements of what would become Advent and Christmas made their appearance. A more complex calendar of worship necessitated an equally complete and rich lectionary.

Evidence of prescribed and organized readings to celebrate the liturgical seasons dates from the fourth century, with patterns showing a mixture of both sequential and selected readings. There was no uniformity among the Churches. Many traditions favored three readings at the Sunday Eucharist, one from the Old Testament, one from the apostolic writings, and one from the gospels. Some traditions had four, five, even six different readings on Sunday. For example, the *Apostolic Constitutions* (most probably written in Syria c. 380) mentions that on Sunday the assembly would hear five readings: a selection each from the Law, the Prophets, the epistles, Acts of the Apostles, and the gospels.

In the fourth and fifth centuries, lectionaries, in the sense of separate books containing prescribed selections from scripture, had yet to make their appearance. Instead, people read directly from a copy of the Bible. They knew which texts to read because the manuscripts of the Bible used at the liturgy featured markings in the margins, called *incipits* and *explicits*, indicating the beginning and the end of the excerpt to be read. Some manuscripts had lists of *incipits* and *explicits*, called a *capitulare*, written at the front or at the back of the codex (book)—a sort of table indicating the prescribed selections for entire liturgical seasons.

It was only in the sixth and seventh centuries that actual "books containing full texts of lessons arranged calendrically" began to proliferate.[11] These early lectionaries were called *comites* (in the singular, a *comes*, Latin

[11] J. Reumann, "A History of Lectionaries: From the Synagogue at Nazareth to Post-Vatican II," *Interpretation* 31 (1977) 116–30.

for "companion") because such books accompanied presiders and cele-brants in their liturgical functions. They were a form of "user-friendly" liturgical Bible—instead of carrying around a copy of the entire Bible, a presider needed only a book or two containing the assigned passages. Some of these *comites*, called evangelaries, collected only gospel readings; others, called epistolaries, contained passages drawn only from the epis-tles; yet other *comites* included both epistle and gospel excerpts. As a rule, *comites* primarily contained the readings specially selected for the major feasts of the liturgical year. For the "green" Sundays, or Sundays of the Year, some *comites* offered a collection of readings from which the presider selected a few for each Sunday.

The Middle Ages

During the Middle Ages the liturgy in western and northern Europe underwent dramatic changes. "Progressive privatization" is perhaps the best way to characterize the overall tendency of liturgical change in this period. For a number of complex reasons, the Eucharist became more and more a ritual reserved entirely for the priest alone with the assembled community reduced to passive onlookers.[12] In great part this was due to the retention of Latin that, as the centuries moved on, fewer and fewer people could speak. After the fall of the Roman Empire, Latin rapidly evolved into vernaculars such as Italian, French, and Spanish. The numer-ous tribes in the northern territories had their own Germanic-based lan-guages. Maintaining Latin in the liturgy helped create a unified worship throughout Europe, but at the cost of fostering an aura of impenetrable mystification. Unless they were educated, people in the assembly did not understand what was being said.

The priest presided with his back to the people. He read the assigned scriptural passages in a low voice in Latin, and he whispered the sacred words of the Eucharistic Prayer to himself. Since the priest did everything, there was no longer any need for a variety of ministries such as lector, can-tor, and eucharistic minister. This priestly monopoly in the liturgy was re-flected in the development of the missal, a book which contained not only the prayers the priest recited, but also the parts once sung by the cantor and the readings originally proclaimed by the lector.

---

[12]See, for example, Joseph A. Jungmann, *The Mass of the Roman Rite: Its Origins and Development*, vol. I, trans. Francis A. Brunner (Dublin: Four Courts Press, 1986 [1948 German original]) 103–59; Johannes H. Emminghaus, *The Eucharist: Essence, Form, Celebration*, trans. Matthew J. O'Connell (Collegeville: The Liturgical Press, 1978) 70–89.

The sense of a liturgical year faded into ever greater obscurity. The addition of Masses on all the weekdays, the proliferation of private votive Masses, the growing number of saints' days—all of these factors conspired to deprive the Sunday of its preeminent position as the original Christian feast day celebrating the paschal mystery. As a result, the liturgical year, which was anchored in and had evolved out of the Sunday celebration, also lost its distinct form and order.

As always, the Lectionary reflects the state of the liturgy. By the end of the Middle Ages, the Lectionary was totally absorbed into the missal and became the province of the priest alone. Many prescribed readings were reassigned; traditional Sunday readings were relegated to weekdays; saints' day readings replaced Sunday readings; the practice of sequential reading fell away. Already by the seventh century, the Old Testament readings had been eliminated almost totally. Clearly there was need for reform. Unfortunately, efforts at reforming the liturgy were too little and came too late.

The Missale Romanum *of 1570*

In its concern to counter the effects of the Protestant Reformation, the Council of Trent (1545–1563) had many more pressing issues to deal with than the liturgy. Nevertheless, the council attempted some liturgical reform, such as stemming the tide of the ever-increasing number of saints' days. In response to the challenge which the Reformation presented, however, Rome ultimately froze the liturgy against what the authorities feared would be further erosion. In 1570 Pope Pius V promulgated the Roman Missal and imposed it as the standard for Roman Catholic liturgy the world over. This missal, which pretty much remained the unchanging norm until the reform of Vatican II, contained not only the prayers for the presider but also all of the scriptural passages assigned for eucharistic celebrations in all possible contexts.

In order to appreciate fully the magnitude of the Vatican II reform of the Lectionary, it is instructive to compare the new Lectionary with the Lectionary which preceded it, that is, with the Lectionary contained in the *Missale Romanum* of 1570. The following table lists the readings found in the 1955 edition of the Roman Missal, which, except for such feasts as Christ the King and the Holy Family, substantially reproduces the tradition of 1570. An asterisk indicates that the passage appears in the newly-revised Sunday Lectionary.

SUNDAY AND FEAST DAY READINGS IN THE
ROMAN MISSAL BEFORE VATICAN II

	Epistle	Gospel
First Sunday of Advent	Romans 13:11-14*	Luke 21:25-33*
Second Sunday of Advent	Romans 15:4-13*	Matthew 11:2-10*
Third Sunday of Advent	Philippians 4:4-7*	John 1:19-28*
Fourth Sunday of Advent	1 Corinthians 4:1-5*	Luke 3:1-6*
Christmas, midnight	Titus 2:11-15*	Luke 2:1-14*
dawn	Titus 3:4-7*	Luke 2:15-20*
day	Hebrews 1:1-12*	John 1:1-14*
Sunday in Christmas Octave	Galatians 4:1-7*	Luke 2:33-40*
Circumcision (New Year)	Titus 2:11-15*	Luke 2:21*
Sunday after Circumcision (Holy Name)	Acts 4:8-12*	Luke 2:21*
Epiphany	Isaiah 60:1-6*	Matthew 2:1-12*
Sunday after Epiphany (Holy Family)	Colossians 3:12-17*	Luke 2:42-52*
Second Sunday after Epiphany	Romans 12:6-16	John 2:1-11*
Third Sunday after Epiphany	Romans 12:16-21	Matthew 8:1-13
Fourth Sunday after Epiphany	Romans 13:8-10	Matthew 8:23-27
Fifth Sunday after Epiphany	Colossians 3:12-17*	Matthew 13:24-30*
Sixth Sunday after Epiphany	1 Thessalonians 1:2-10	Matthew 13:31-35
Septuagesima	1 Corinthians 9:24–10:5*	Matthew 20:1-16*
Sexagesima	2 Corinthians 11:19–12:9	Luke 8:4-15
Quinquagesima	1 Corinthians 13:1-13	Luke 18:31-43*
First Sunday of Lent	2 Corinthians 6:1-10*	Matthew 4:1-11*
Second Sunday of Lent	1 Thessalonians 4:1-7	Matthew 17:1-9*
Third Sunday of Lent	Ephesians 5:1-9	Luke 11:14-28
Fourth Sunday of Lent	Galatians 4:22-31	John 6:1-15*
Passion Sunday	Hebrews 9:11-15*	John 8:46-59
Palm Sunday	Philippians 2:5-11*	Matthew 26:1–27:66*
Holy Thursday	1 Corinthians 11:20-32*	John 13:1-15*
Good Friday	Hosea 6:1-6	
	Exodus 12:1-11*	John 18:1-40; 19:1-42*
Easter Vigil	Genesis 1:1-22; 2:1-2*	

SUNDAY AND FEAST DAY READINGS IN THE
ROMAN MISSAL BEFORE VATICAN II *(Cont'd)*

	Epistle	Gospel
	Genesis 5–8	
	Genesis 22:1-19*	
	Exodus 14:24-31; 15:1*	
	Isaiah 54:17; 55:1-11*	
	Baruch 3:9-38*	
	Ezekiel 37:1-14*	
	Isaiah 4:1-6	
	Exodus 12:1-11*	
	Jonah 3:1-10	
	Deuteronomy 31:22-30	
	Daniel 3:1-14	
	Colossians 3:1-4*	Matthew 28:1-7*
Easter	1 Corinthians 5:7-8*	Mark 16:1-7*
First Sunday after Easter	1 John 5:4-10*	John 20:19-31*
Second Sunday after Easter	1 Peter 2:21-25*	John 10:11-16*
Third Sunday after Easter	1 Peter 2:11-19	John 16:16-22
Fourth Sunday after Easter	James 1:17-21*	John 16:5-14
Fifth Sunday after Easter	James 1:22-27	John 16:23-30
Ascension	Acts 1:1-11*	Mark 16:14-20*
Sunday after Ascension	1 Peter 4:7-11	John 15:26–16:4
Pentecost	Acts 2:1-11*	John 14:23-31*
First Sunday after Pentecost	Romans 11:33-36*	Matthew 28:18-20*
Second Sunday after Pentecost	1 John 3:13-18	Luke 14:16-24
Third Sunday after Pentecost	1 Peter 5:6-11	Luke 15:1-10*
Fourth Sunday after Pentecost	Romans 8:18-23	Luke 5:1-11*
Fifth Sunday after Pentecost	1 Peter 3:8-15	Matthew 5:20-24
Sixth Sunday after Pentecost	Romans 6:3-11*	Mark 8:1-9
Seventh Sunday after Pentecost	Romans 6:19-23	Matthew 7:15-21
Eighth Sunday after Pentecost	Romans 8:12-17	Luke 16:1-9*

SUNDAY AND FEAST DAY READINGS IN THE
ROMAN MISSAL BEFORE VATICAN II *(Cont'd)*

	Epistle	Gospel
Ninth Sunday after Pentecost	1 Corinthians 10:6-13	Luke 19:41-47
Tenth Sunday after Pentecost	1 Corinthians 12:2-11*	Luke 18:9-14*
Eleventh Sunday after Pentecost	1 Corinthians 15:1-10*	Mark 7:31-37*
Twelfth Sunday after Pentecost	2 Corinthians 3:4-9	Luke 10:23-37*
Thirteenth Sunday after Pentecost	Galatians 3:16-22	Luke 17:11-19*
Fourteenth Sunday after Pentecost	Galatians 5:16-24*	Matthew 6:24-33*
Fifteenth Sunday after Pentecost	Galatians 5:25–6:10	Luke 7:11-16*
Sixteenth Sunday after Pentecost	Ephesians 3:13-21*	Luke 14:1-11
Seventeenth Sunday after Pentecost	Ephesians 4:1-6*	Matthew 22:34-46*
Eighteenth Sunday after Pentecost	1 Corinthians 1:4-8*	Matthew 9:1-8
Nineteenth Sunday after Pentecost	Ephesians 4:23-28	Matthew 22:1-14*
Twentieth Sunday after Pentecost	Ephesians 5:15-21*	John 4:46-53
Twenty-first Sunday after Pentecost	Ephesians 6:10-17	Matthew 18:23-35
Twenty-second Sunday after Pentecost	Philippians 1:6-11*	Matthew 22:15-21*
Twenty-third Sunday after Pentecost	Philippians 3:17–4:3*	Matthew 9:18-26
Last Sunday after Pentecost	Colossians 1:9-14	Matthew 24:15-35
(Last Sunday in October Christ the King	Colossians 1:12-20*	John 18:33-37*)

A rapid perusal of this list points out the following salient characteristics of the Sunday and Feast Day Lectionary contained in the 1955 edition of the 1570 *Missale Romanum*:

- It was organized in a one-year cycle, containing a total of 138 different biblical passages.

- With the exception of the Easter vigil (celebrated early on the morning of Holy Saturday until the reforms of Pius XII in 1951), each Sunday and Feast Day had two readings: the first, called the Epistle, was selected, with only three exceptions, from the New Testament letters; the second, called the Gospel, was an excerpt from one of the four gospels.

- The Old Testament was read on only three occasions: on the Feast of the Epiphany, on Good Friday, and at the Easter vigil.

- Passages from Mark's gospel appeared on only four occasions, while excerpts from Matthew and Luke were assigned to twenty-two and twenty-one Sundays and Feast Days respectively. John was read primarily during the Easter Season (fourteen passages), with a few passages scattered at Christmas and in Lent.

- There were only three excerpts from Acts of the Apostles (on the Sunday after Circumcision, on Ascension, and on Pentecost), nothing at all from Second Thessalonians or from Revelation.

- The liturgical year had two festal cycles (Advent-Christmas and Lent-Easter), but the Sundays of the Year were not always clearly defined. For example, between the end of the Advent-Christmas season and the beginning of the Lent-Easter season came "Sundays after Epiphany," as though they were a continuation of the feast. Septuagesima Sunday, Sexagesima Sunday, and Quinquagesima Sunday anticipated the season of Lent in a kind of mini-Lent before Lent. The Sundays between Easter and Pentecost were called "Sundays *after* Easter" rather than "Sundays *of* Easter" as in the current liturgy, while the Sundays between Pentecost and the following Advent were called "Sundays after Pentecost" instead of the current "Sundays in Ordinary Time."

- There were but two minor instances of sequential reading for the gospels (the midnight and dawn Masses of Christmas, the Third Sunday after Epiphany through to Septuagesima Sunday), and a number of short sequences for the epistles (the midnight and dawn Masses of Christmas, the Second to Fourth Sundays after Epiphany, the Fourth and Fifth Sundays after Easter, and several sequences from the Sixth to the last Sunday after Pentecost). With the exception of the Eighteenth Sunday, from the Sixth to the

Twenty-fourth Sundays after Pentecost there was a (broadly-defined) semicontinuous reading of the Pauline epistles in that they were read in the order found in the New Testament. For the major solemnities the readings were selected to reflect the feast being celebrated. The selections of gospel readings during the festal seasons, based on ancient tradition, expressed the significance of the seasons, but during the Sundays of the year the readings had no perceivable pattern.

• All the scripture readings were contained in the Roman Missal (no separate Lectionary book) and they were all read in Latin by the priest (no ministry of lector).

Such was the state of the Sunday and Feast Day Lectionary that Vatican II sought to ameliorate. How the council proceeded in its reform of the Lectionary is the topic of the next chapter.

2 The Vatican II Reform of the Lectionary

The preceding chapter offered a survey of the history of Lectionaries from the ancient Jewish synagogue up to the Roman Missal of 1570. This chapter describes the latest installment in the continuing history of Lectionaries, that of the Vatican II reform. The next chapter will review in some detail the major decisions of the conciliar committee that edited the new Lectionary.

Historical Context of the Vatican II Lectionary Reform

The revision of the Lectionary is but a small part of a much wider renewal of the liturgy; the reform of the liturgy in turn is one facet of the renewal of the whole Church effected by Vatican II. In order to appreciate the current Lectionary, it is necessary to examine the work of revision in its historical context.

Although Pope John XXIII's call for an ecumenical council on January 25, 1959, came as a total surprise, the full-scale renewal of the Church which resulted had been in preparation for decades, both in the writings of scholars and in the *praxis* of communities throughout the world who keenly felt the need for change. Among the wishes for change, a desired reform of the Lectionary had surfaced above all in three fields of study and experience, all of which trace their origins back to the end of the last century: biblical studies, the liturgical movement, and the catechetical movement.[1]

The rise of critical biblical scholarship in Catholic circles led to a rediscovery of the riches contained in the Bible as a whole. In light of this,

---

[1] This section presents a summary of material found in Elmar Nübold, *Entstehung und Bewertung der neuen Perikopenordnung des Römischen Ritus für die Messfeier an Sonn- und Festtagen* (Paderborn: Verlag Bonifatius-Druckerei, 1986) 19–43.

the traditional use of scripture as a source of prooftexts for doctrine began to appear more and more narrow and inadequate. The rediscovery of the riches of scripture also made people realize the limited scope of the Sunday and Feast Day readings contained in the Roman Missal of 1570. As a result, many Catholics—scholars, clergy, laypeople—began to demand that a broader and more representative selection of biblical passages, from both the Old and New Testaments, be offered to the liturgical assembly.

New research in the history of liturgy demonstrated the centrality of Sunday and the importance of the liturgical seasons in the ancient Church. Together, these aspects of early Church tradition pointed to the paschal mystery of Christ as the prime focus of Christian liturgy. As well, scholars noticed that ancient liturgy, steeped in the scriptures, turned to them as the source *par excellence* for proclaiming this mystery and that the primary moment for its proclamation was at the celebration of the Eucharist. Many hoped fervently, therefore, that the intimate relationship between liturgy and scripture, so characteristic of the early Church, might once again be actively fostered in church.

Voices for the reform of the Lectionary in the realm of catechetics were raised in Europe as well as in missionary lands. Pastors found that, since the Sunday Lectionary was so intimately linked with the Eucharist, it constituted a prime source of evangelization and instruction. However, it was disappointingly poor due to the limited number of biblical passages it contained. Preachers who were more attuned to the biblical dimension of liturgy also felt that the Lectionary of the Roman Missal offered too narrow a selection of readings from which to work.

In each of these fields, scholars presented, debated, and published proposals for Lectionary reform, laying a broad and solid foundation for the council's revision. The committee which implemented the Vatican II renewal of the Lectionary chose its members from these movements and drew much of its inspiration from their various studies.

Chronology of the Vatican II Lectionary Reform[2]

Before officially convoking the council, Pope John XXIII named a special commission whose task it was to consult Church leaders through-

---

[2]The information contained in this section is drawn for the most part from E. Nübold, *Entstehung*, 115–70; Annibale Bugnini, *The Reform of the Liturgy 1948–1975*, trans. Matthew O'Connell (Collegeville: The Liturgical Press, 1990 [1983]) 14–28, 406–25; and Gaston Fontaine, "Commentarium ad Ordinem Lectionum Missae," *Notitiae* 5 (1969) 256–82.

out the world about their desires for reform. On May 17, 1959, this commission sent to 2,594 bishops and prelates, 156 superiors of religious orders, and 62 theological institutes a questionnaire about their wishes for Church renewal. By May 1960, 2,150 responses were returned to Rome, of which about 25 percent addressed liturgical matters. Of these 500 or so responses on the liturgy, about 150 specifically mentioned the renewal of the Lectionary. For the most part, these responses on the Lectionary voiced the biblical, liturgical, and catechetical concerns mentioned above.

Next, between June 1961 and June 1962, a preparatory commission sorted through all the information gathered by this special commission and then drafted the data into documents which were to be debated at the council itself. In the meantime, on Christmas Day 1961, Pope John XXIII officially convoked the council.

The council itself met in four sessions between October 11, 1962, and December 8, 1965. No documents were approved during the first session (October 11 to December 8, 1962), for the Council Fathers did not deem the early drafts to be adequate. During the second session (September 29 to December 4, 1963), they set to work on the draft of the document on liturgy. After many revisions and much debate, on the last day of the session the assembly of bishops voted on and approved their first document, the Constitution on the Sacred Liturgy (*Sacrosanctum Concilium*).

The Constitution on the Sacred Liturgy was designed "to serve as a guide in the renewal of the liturgy of God's people."[3] It did not elaborate on the specifics of liturgical reform, but rather set forth the basic principles guiding it. In order to implement the liturgical reforms the constitution mandated, in January 1964 the council established a committee called a *Consilium*. At its first meeting on March 11, 1964, the *Consilium* on liturgy formed forty working groups called *coeti* in Latin, one of which, *Coetus XI*, was assigned the task of Lectionary reform. The entire *Consilium* with its committees met thirteen times between 1964 and 1970. Votes on the new Lectionary took place during the fourth, seventh, and tenth plenary sessions.

The committee for the revision of the Lectionary was composed of eighteen permanent members divided into two categories: consultors named by the Holy See and *consilarii* named by the president of the committee. In addition, each committee also had a secretary. For *Coetus XI* the roll call of members is as follows: president, C. Vagaggini (Italy); secretary, G. Fontaine (Canada); consultors: P. Jounel (France), P. Massi (Italy), A.

---

[3] A. Bugnini, *The Reform of the Liturgy*, 39.

Rose (Belgium), G. Diekmann (U.S.A.), E. Lanne (Belgium), A. Nocent (Belgium), A.-M. Roguet (France), J. Feder (France), H. Kahlefeld (Germany), K. Tillmann (Germany); *consilarii*, H. Schürmann (Germany), H. Oster (France), J. Gaillard (France), H. Marot (Belgium), L. Deiss (France), C. Wiéner (France). In all, the committee held fourteen sessions between September 1964 and February 1969. Thirty years after the council, the strengths and limitations of this roster have become more apparent. While comprising the most illustrious scholars available to effect Lectionary reform, the list shows that *Coetus XI* was composed of European men (only two members from North America, none from Asia, Africa, or Latin America), and that French was the dominant language. The revised Lectionary, then, reflects the state of the Church and of theological scholarship in the 1960s.

Despite such limitations, the revised Lectionary is a noteworthy achievement. Never before in the history of Christian liturgy had such a thorough revision of the Lectionary been undertaken. Historical research based on newly-discovered ancient liturgical manuscripts and carried out with the help of new methods and technologies fostered an understanding of liturgy and of liturgical history that had simply not been possible in previous centuries. The time was indeed ripe for a fully-informed effort to reform the Lectionary according to solid liturgical principles founded on ancient tradition.

Five Principles Guiding Lectionary Reform

In fact, no separate section in the Constitution on the Sacred Liturgy deals specifically with the Lectionary. However, scattered throughout the document, as well as in the related document the Constitution on Divine Revelation (*Dei Verbum*), are numerous comments that express the wishes of the council regarding Lectionary reform. Elmar Nübold distills these comments into five main principles that together guided the work of the post-conciliar committee on the Lectionary.[4]

The five principles are listed below. In addition, passages quoted from the council documents accompany each principle in order to give a sample of the type of statements that inspired it. Because of the nature of documents, the language and tone of the citations are at times solemn and stilted, but their tenor is always clear.

[4]E. Nübold, *Entstehung*, 172–7.

1. The scriptures are an essential component of liturgical celebration.

The importance of the scriptures for the celebration of the liturgy is a broad principle. It contains a number of facets expressed in several related ways:

a. Scripture is the source of liturgy: "The importance of scripture in the celebration of the liturgy is paramount. For it is texts from scripture that form the readings and are explained in the homily; it is scripture's psalms that are sung; from scripture's inspiration and influence flow the various kinds of prayers as well as the singing in the liturgy; from scripture the actions and signs derive their meaning" (*SC*, no. 24).[5]

b. Christ is present in scripture: "[Christ] is present through his word, in that he himself is speaking when scripture is read in church" (*SC*, no. 7). "The church has always held the divine scriptures in reverence no less than it accords to the Lord's body itself, never ceasing—especially in the sacred liturgy—to receive the bread of life from the one table of God's word and Christ's body, and to offer it to the faithful" (*DV*, no. 21).

c. Scripture is a source of instruction: "Although the liturgy is primarily the worship of the divine majesty, it contains also a large element of instruction for the believers who form the congregation . . . . And so, it is not just when the things which 'are written for our instruction' (Rom 15:4) are read out, but also while the church is singing, praying or performing, that the faith of those taking part is nourished and their minds raised to God, enabling them to give him free and conscious service and to receive his grace more abundantly" (*SC*, no. 33).

d. Since scripture is an integral part of the eucharistic celebrations, there is need for a better selection of passages: "In order that believers can be provided with a richer diet of God's word, the rich heritage of the Bible is to be opened more widely, in such a way that a fuller and more nourishing selection of the scriptures gets read to the people within a fixed period of years" (*SC*, no. 51). "In liturgical celebrations, a fuller, more varied and more appropriate approach to the reading of scripture is to be restored" (*SC*, no. 35.1).

---

[5]The translation of *Sacrosanctum Concilium* used throughout this book is that of Philip Endean, found in Norman P. Tanner, ed. *Decrees of the Ecumenical Councils. Vol. 2: Trent to Vatican II* (London: Sheed & Ward / Washington, D.C.: Georgetown University Press, 1990) 820–43. The translation of *Dei Verbum* was made by Robert Murray, published in the same volume, 971–81.

2. Priority is to be given to the Sunday and Feast Day Lectionary.

This axiom flows from the research showing the importance of Sunday and of the liturgical seasons in the ancient Church. These key aspects of liturgy had become progressively more obscured from late antiquity through to the end of the Middle Ages, a state of affairs not ameliorated by the promulgation of the Roman Missal of 1570. The Constitution on the Sacred Liturgy expresses the role of Sundays and Feast Days in such phrases as: "For on this day, christian believers should come together, in order to commemorate the suffering, resurrection and glory of the lord Jesus, by hearing God's word and sharing the Eucharist . . ." (*SC*, no. 106); ". . . taking account of Masses celebrated with the people present, particularly on Sundays and holydays of obligation" (*SC*, no. 49).

Although the Constitution mentions liturgical seasons only in passing (*SC*, no. 107), the history of liturgy provides ample evidence that the liturgical year evolved out of the Sunday eucharistic celebration. By concentrating on Sundays, Feast Days of the Lord, and liturgical seasons, the council sought to sweep away centuries of accretions that had cluttered the liturgy's core realities. Whatever prevented people from perceiving and experiencing the liturgy as a celebration of the mystery of Christ, of his death and resurrection as the fulfillment of salvation history, was to be removed.

3. The Lectionary is to contain more scripture.

The Lectionary is to contain the more representative or essential parts (*praestantior pars* in Latin) of the scriptures. Realizing that it would be both impossible and inappropriate to read every part of every book of the scriptures at liturgy (for example, the purity laws of Leviticus, the long descriptions of the Ark of the Covenant in Exodus, the violent stories in Judges, etc.), the writers of the Constitution on the Sacred Liturgy proposed three criteria for selecting the "essential" or "most important" part of scripture: (1) focus on Christ as (2) the center and fulfillment of salvation history (3) proclaimed for Christian life.

> *First Criterion:* Christ is the focus of each liturgical celebration, particularly of the Sunday assembly when Christians commemorate his death and resurrection in the Eucharist. But this mystery of Christ is so rich that the Church celebrates different aspects of it in its seasons of Advent-Christmas and Lent-Easter: "Moreover, the church unfolds the whole

mystery of Christ over the cycle of the year, from his incarnation and birth to his return to heaven, to the day of Pentecost, and to our waiting for our hope of bliss and the return of the Lord" (*SC*, no. 102).

Second Criterion: Christ is the fulfillment of salvation history. Hence, the readings at the Eucharist are to express the place of Christ in God's plan of salvation. This criterion intends the introduction of Old Testament readings at the Sunday and Feast Day Eucharists: "The great divine acts among the people of the old covenant foreshadowed this deed of human redemption and perfect glorification of God; Christ the lord brought it to its completion, above all through the paschal mystery, that is, his passion, his resurrection from the dead and his glorious ascension" (*SC*, no. 5).

Third Criterion: The Lectionary is to contain texts which allow homilists to expound "the guiding principles of the christian life" (*SC*, no. 52). This concern comes from the realization that "[l]iturgy is not the only activity of the church" (*SC*, no. 9). Celebrating the liturgy must be supplemented with instruction on how to appropriate and actualize the paschal mystery, that the faithful might be transformed ever more profoundly by the life, death and resurrection of the Lord.

These criteria flow from the *liturgical* context of the use of scripture. In the specific instance of the Sunday and Feast Day Lectionary, the liturgical context is that of the *Sunday eucharistic* celebration. This Sunday and Feast Day Lectionary, then, is totally determined by and is fully at the service of the Sunday eucharistic liturgy.

4. The Lectionary is to be adapted to modern times.

The pastoral care of the Church was one of the major thrusts of the entire council, expressed so well in the Italian word *aggiornamento*— "bringing up-to-date." Although there is no explicit reference to this kind of up-dating specifically for the Lectionary, the Constitution on the Sacred Liturgy expresses its desires for the reform of the liturgy as a whole in such phrases as: ". . . that the very design of the rites may make a contribution towards bringing about the full pastoral effect of the sacrifice of the mass . . ." (*SC*, no. 49); ". . . this holy council . . . wants [the rites] to be revised in the light of sound tradition, and to be given new vigour in order to meet today's circumstances and needs" (*SC*, no. 4); "The liturgical year is to be revised. The traditional customs and practices of the liturgical seasons are to be preserved or restored, in line with the circumstances of our time" (*SC*, no. 107); "The general laws regarding the structure and intention of the liturgy should also be taken into account, as well as the experience stemming from more recent liturgical renewal and from the special concessions that have, from time to time, been granted" (*SC*, no. 23; also nos. 37–40).

5. The Lectionary is to take into account previous tradition.

Again, nothing on this topic in the Constitution on the Sacred Liturgy directly addresses the Lectionary. What applies, however, to the liturgical renewal in general necessarily includes the Lectionary as well, for the Lectionary is part of liturgy. The council's wish that the revised liturgy be closely connected to tradition is expressed this way: "In order that healthy tradition can be preserved while yet allowing room for legitimate development, thorough investigation—theological, historical and pastoral—of individual parts of the liturgy up for revision is always to be the first step . . . . care should be taken to see that new forms grow in some way organically out of the forms already existing" (*SC*, no. 23); ". . . faithfully in accordance with the tradition" (*SC*, no. 4). "The liturgical year is to be revised. The traditional customs and practices of the liturgical seasons are to be preserved or restored, in line with the circumstances of our time. Their basic thrust is to be retained, so that they nourish as they should people's religious observance in celebrating the mysteries of christian redemption—above all the easter [paschal] mystery" (*SC*, no. 107).

Coetus XI

Guided by the above principles gleaned from the council documents, the members of *Coetus XI*, who had been assigned the task of Lectionary reform, set to work. As a first order of business, the committee reviewed all the Latin Lectionaries from the sixth to the twelfth centuries, the Lectionaries of fifteen oriental rites, and all the Lectionaries then in use by Protestant Churches. This resulted in over fifty different tables representing almost eighteen centuries of eucharistic Lectionaries. Added to this, the members gathered all the research that had been done in the previous eighty years on the history of liturgy, especially as it was germane to the history of Lectionaries. Finally, they studied the various suggestions for Lectionary reform proposed during the preceding decades by scholars in the three fields mentioned earlier: biblical studies, the liturgical movement, and the catechetical movement.

The next step in the task of *Coetus XI* was to invite thirty-one biblical scholars to submit lists of the scriptural passages they considered to be the most important for reading at the Sunday eucharistic liturgy. They were also asked to specify in which season or on which feast such passages should be read. From these lists the members of *Coetus XI* prepared a consolidated list that they sent to about one hundred catechetical experts and pastors for their comments. In addition to gathering information, the members of the committee contributed special studies on various Lectionary traditions and submitted proposals for revision. All of these tasks went on simultaneously in the years 1964 to 1967, the period during which the committee accomplished the bulk of its work.

Finally, before submitting a final product to the *Consilium* and ultimately for the Pope's approval, the committee added yet one more step. In 1967 they distributed to some eight hundred biblical scholars, liturgists, pastoral theologians, and catechists a draft of the new Lectionary for their evaluation. This resulted in over four hundred pages of general comments and nearly seven thousand notes on specific texts in the Lectionary. In light of the responses, the committee made revisions such as introducing an Old Testament salvation history sequence through the first five Sundays of Lent; adding important passages from the Old Testament to the Sundays in Ordinary Time, even if they did not "correspond" narrowly with the gospel passage of the day; and giving greater prominence to what is unique in each of the three synoptic gospels in their respective years.

On April 3, 1969, Pope Paul VI approved the revised *Lectionary for Mass*, officially promulgated it on May 29, 1969, and declared it mandatory for the entire Roman Catholic Church beginning on November 28, 1971, the First Sunday of Advent. In 1981, a slightly revised edition was issued. The changes are mostly in the form of the addition of texts in Years B and C for a number of feasts.

3   The Work of *Coetus XI*

The Constitution on the Sacred Liturgy couched its desires for the revision of the Lectionary in the general terms of guiding principles. The task of implementing the council's wishes fell to the members of *Coetus XI*, the *Consilium* committee on Lectionary reform. Within the space of three years (1964–1967), they had succeeded in designing the Lectionary that has since become a prominent feature of the Sunday Eucharist.

This chapter presents the major characteristics of the Sunday and Feast Day Lectionary, along with sketches of some of the issues which the members of *Coetus XI* discussed en route to their decisions. The sequence of topics treated here does not necessarily follow the order in which the committee dealt with them; as in a tapestry, the many threads are interwoven.

The Paschal Mystery as Unifying Theme

The first and most important characteristic of the Sunday and Feast Day Lectionary is its orientation to the paschal mystery of Jesus' death and resurrection. This follows from the fact that the Lectionary is a repertoire of biblical passages to be read in the liturgical context of the *Sunday Eucharist.*

The type and frequency of a community's worship determines the shape and content of the Lectionary. The same principle holds, of course, for the Lectionary for the Sunday Eucharist. Because Sunday is the day of the Lord, the day on which he rose from the dead, the day signalling the inauguration of God's eschatological reign, Christians established it from the very beginning as the preeminent time to hold their eucharistic assemblies. And of all the Church's liturgical actions, the Eucharist remains the preeminent celebration of the paschal mystery. From at least the middle of the second century, these Sunday eucharistic gatherings included the reading of scripture.

The 1981 edition of the Introduction to the *Lectionary for Mass* clearly expresses the relationship between the word of God and the paschal mystery as celebrated in the Eucharist, especially the Sunday Eucharist, when it states:

> It can never be forgotten, therefore, that the divine word read and pro-claimed by the Church in the liturgy has as its one goal the sacrifice of the New Covenant and the banquet of grace, that is, the eucharist. The celebration of Mass in which the word is heard and the eucharist is of-fered and received forms but one single act of divine worship (*SC*, no. 56). That act offers the sacrifice of praise to God and makes available to God's creatures the fullness of redemption (no. 10).[1]

It stands to reason, therefore, that the Sunday Lectionary, being an essen-tial component of such a highly Christocentric setting as the Sunday Eucharist, should find its center in the paschal mystery.

The Sunday Lectionary's fundamental focus on the paschal mystery entails important consequences. William Skudlarek explains that the committee, in designing the Lectionary as it did,

> . . . rejected, at least implicitly, other ways of going about its task. The lectionary was not to be ordered around a "history of salvation" motif (understood as a line running from the creation to the second coming), or around a systematic presentation of the theological teachings of the church, or according to a literary analysis of the parts of the Bible that were to be used. Nor were the readings to be chosen and ordered for the primary purpose of exhorting and encouraging people to lead more Christian lives. The lectionary was there to proclaim the passion, death, resurrection, and ascension of Christ, fully realized in him and being realized in us who, through faith and baptism, have been joined to him.[2]

Accordingly, then, liturgical principles take precedence over exegeti-cal, catechetical, paraenetic or other principles in determining the selec-tion and distribution of biblical passages in the Sunday Lectionary. This is because the liturgy is concerned with the community here and now as-sembled. The story which the liturgy celebrates is salvation history actu-alized in the present, where the past and the future meet as memory and

---

[1] This and all other citations of the 1981 Introduction to the *Lectionary for Mass* are taken from the ICEL translation found in *The Liturgy Documents: A Parish Resource*, Third Edition, ed. Elizabeth Hoffman (Chicago: Liturgy Training Publications, 1991) 127–64.

[2] William Skudlarek, *The Word in Worship: Preaching in a Liturgical Context* (Nashville: Abingdon, 1981) 33–4.

anticipation. Liturgy brings to its most self-conscious and intense expression the current chapter of the story of salvation happening at this time and place in the lives of the gathered worshippers.

Liturgy is the ritualization of the on-going drama of the relationship between the faithful and their risen Lord who configures them into the pattern of his death and resurrection. The liturgical year groups Sundays and Feast Days into liturgical seasons. Each liturgical season stresses a particular aspect of this "narrative." The season of Lent tells the story of conversion and repentance culminating in the believers' appropriation of the paschal mystery through baptism and Eucharist at the Easter vigil. The Easter season celebrates the story of the deepening communion of the faithful with the risen Lord who abides with his Church through the Spirit. The Advent-Christmas season unfolds the story of the community's patient waiting for the fullness of the kingdom still to come, a time of commemoration and anticipation which they fill with purposeful action until the fullness of the paschal mystery is revealed in them. The Sundays in Ordinary Time actualize the story of Christians being shaped and molded into Jesus' death and resurrection through the difficult fidelity of discipleship. In each instance the readings selected for the Sunday Lectionary articulate and celebrate these liturgical "narratives." Thus, the Sunday Eucharist, which celebrates the paschal mystery, and the liturgical year, every aspect of which flows from and points to the paschal mystery of Christ, together fully determine the shape and content of the Sunday Lectionary.

Sculpted by its eucharistic setting and by the liturgical year, the Sunday and Feast Day Lectionary does not for all that remain a passive liturgical artifact. While the liturgy of the Eucharist remains substantially the same from celebration to celebration, the stories and images proclaimed in the biblical selections sound distinctive notes that send echoes through the Eucharistic Prayer, making the paschal mystery reverberate in various modes and keys according to feast and season. The biblical passages read on Sundays and Feast Days subtly accentuate even the eucharistic meal itself. Lenten communion contains a trace of the bread of affliction, the cup, a tinge of bitterness and gall. At Eastertide, the bread and wine hint of the sweetness of the heavenly banquet. Advent's eucharistic table is seasoned with a touch of impatience and anticipation. The weekly repast during Ordinary Time tastes of the solid sustenance of food for the journey. The Lectionary actively defines and shapes the Church's celebrations of the paschal mystery.

Continuity and Discontinuity: The Roman Missal of 1570

Since the Constitution on the Sacred Liturgy explicitly recommended that the revised Sunday and Feast Day Lectionary be organized in a multi-year cycle, the members of *Coetus XI* had to decide what to do with the one-year cycle Lectionary that Roman Catholics had been using since 1570 (described above in chapter 1). Even if impoverished, this Lectionary nevertheless represented an important strand of tradition. Moreover, the constitution urged that ". . . care should be taken to see that new forms grow in some way organically out of the forms already existing . . .," and be shaped ". . . faithfully in accordance with the tradition" (*SC,* nos. 23 and 4).

Research showed that the Lectionary contained in the Roman Missal of 1570 embodied a Roman tradition reaching back at least to the seventh century, and, in some particulars, as far back as the fifth century. After the Reformation in the sixteenth century, this same Roman Lectionary had served as the basis for a number of Protestant Lectionaries. Perhaps with a few revisions, some committee members argued, it might once again provide a good foundation for a unified, ecumenical Lectionary.

As attractive as this idea appeared at first, the picture was found to be somewhat more complicated. In most cases, Protestant Churches had significantly added to or otherwise altered the original Roman tradition; other Churches had totally abandoned it for a new, multi-year cycle of readings. Moreover, even if this Roman Lectionary constituted a common tradition underlying many Lectionaries, it had not represented a common tradition in antiquity. At that time there was no one recognized order of readings among the Churches.

Even if the Lectionary contained in the Roman Missal of 1570 could not realistically be used as the foundation of an ecumenical order of readings, could it at least be kept as the first year of a multi-year cycle? In this way, continuity with (recent) tradition would be highlighted. However, the inadequacies of the 1570 Lectionary, particularly its not reflecting the prominent place of Sunday and the distinctive pattern of liturgical seasons, would require that it undergo such alterations as to be hardly recognizable. On the other hand, if with only minor revisions it were kept as the first year of a multi-year cycle, the successive years would be forced to follow the structure and pattern of the first year. But the structure and pattern of the 1570 Lectionary were the very features that made it inadequate in the first place. It would be best to construct a multi-year cycle of readings based on a structure and pattern that responded to the wishes of the council and the demands of the reformed liturgy. The 1570 Lectionary, then, could function neither as the basis for a common Lectionary nor as the first year of a multi-year cycle, and so the committee decided it would be best to set it aside and proceed with a total reform.

Although the members of *Coetus XI* opted to effect a total reform of the Lectionary, they nevertheless chose to retain the majority of 1570 Roman Missal readings in the revised Lectionary. Of the 138 passages contained in the pre-Vatican II Sunday and Feast Day Lectionary, at least eighty-five also appear in the current Lectionary.[3] In a sense this comes as no surprise, for the traditional readings on feasts like Christmas and Epiphany, as well as readings during the festal seasons of Advent, Lent, and Easter—biblical passages that either constitute the feast or provide the theme of the season—are as adequate to the task now as they were then. In other instances, readings in the 1570 Lectionary were placed elsewhere in the liturgical year to accommodate the new patterns of the current Lectionary. The editors of the reformed Lectionary, then, reflect Jesus' description of the scribe trained for the kingdom of God: "He is like the master of a household who brings out of his treasure what is new and what is old" (Matt 13:52).

A Three-Year Cycle of Readings

The Constitution on the Sacred Liturgy explicitly recommended that the new Lectionary be structured in a multi-year cycle of readings: "In order that believers can be provided with a richer diet of God's word, the rich heritage of the Bible is to be opened more widely, in such a way that a fuller and more nourishing selection of the scriptures gets read to the people within a fixed period of years" (*SC,* no. 51). However, the document expressed this wish in general terms, leaving the committee the task of dealing with the particulars.

A multi-year cycle assumes, of course, that each year of the cycle will have essentially the same pattern: ". . . the church unfolds the whole mystery of Christ over the cycle of the year, from his incarnation and birth to his return to heaven, to the day of Pentecost, and to our waiting for our hope of bliss and the return of the Lord" (*SC,* no. 102). But the question

---

[3]The list of readings contained in the 1955 edition of the 1570 Roman Missal appears at the end of chapter 1 above. An asterisk indicates that the reading was retained, in whole or in part, in the revised Sunday Lectionary.

remained: a cycle of how many years would best realize the council's de-sire for more scripture in the liturgy?

In reality many interrelated aspects to this question had to be an-swered together. For example, how many years would it take to cover the *praestantior pars* ("the more essential, precious, useful part") of scripture? If the cycle is too short, individual readings would have to be quite long for the Lectionary to include all of the scripture deemed important. If the cycle of years is too long, people's ability to become familiar with passages would be diminished, for familiarity demands some degree of repetition. As well, what pattern or patterns of reading distribution in each year of the cycle would best assure the realization of these two *desiderata*? Whatever these patterns might be, they must be simple yet flexible.

The members of the committee examined and discussed proposals for cycles of two, three, four, and five years. At first, the majority of the committee favored a four-year cycle. In time, however, the three-year pro-posal emerged as the solution best able to respond to the several concerns mentioned above. The committee finally accepted a three-year cycle orga-nized around the designation of a different synoptic gospel for each year of the cycle—Matthew for Year A, Mark for Year B, and Luke for Year C. Simple and elegant, it has left its imprint as perhaps the most immediately recognizable trait of the revised Sunday Lectionary.

Why not a four-year cycle, with a fourth year for John's gospel? There were two main reasons for not doing this, one having to do with tradition, the other with the literary nature of the Fourth Gospel. Ancient tradition privileged John's gospel during Lent, Holy Week, and Eastertide. The members of *Coetus XI* felt it was more important to respect this hallowed tradition than to assign John's gospel its own year. Besides, one of the most distinctive features of this gospel is its long dialogues and discourses, which do not easily lend themselves to being divided into small passages. It would be very difficult, not to mention exegetically unsound, to break the gospel into a sufficient number of small pericopes to fill up an entire year of Sunday gospel readings.

Finally, not only did the three-year cycle best realize the mandate of the council—offer the essential parts of scripture, foster familiarity with scripture, provide a flexible, elegant, and simple structure—it also enjoyed a favored place in many ancient and recent traditions. The Church in Milan instituted a three-year cycle of readings at the end of the fourth century. Soon after, Spain and Gaul adopted the pattern. Rome used it until the fifth century, the Byzantine Church until the seventh century. There were precedents for a three-year cycle of readings in a number of

contemporary Protestant Churches, and the ancient Palestinian synagogue Lectionary cycle of Torah readings also featured a three-year cycle.
Except for assigning a different synoptic gospel to each year of the cycle,
the committee had in a sense invented nothing new.

Advantages of a Three-Year Cycle

In the words of one commentator, "[t]he solution of a three-year
cycle with a Gospel of the year is undoubtedly one of the most successful
features of the lectionary."[4] A three-year cycle presents a greater selection
of scriptural passages. The Roman Missal of 1570 contained in all (in its
1955 version, including the readings at the Easter vigil as well as the texts
for the several Christmas Masses) a total of 138 passages from scripture.
The revised Lectionary offers three readings on each Sunday and Feast
Day over a three-year period for a total of 529 different passages (160 Old
Testament, 369 New Testament).[5]

Each year of the three-year cycle has its own character, determined by
the synoptic gospel assigned to it. In Year A the Lectionary offers
Matthew's portrait of Jesus as teacher and preacher who announces the
Good News of the Kingdom of Heaven; in Year B the Lectionary presents
the Marcan Jesus as a man of God who confronts and overcomes the powers of illness, sin, and death; in Year C the Lectionary proposes the Lucan
Jesus who, in his seeking out the poor and the outcast, reveals God's mercy
and compassion. Designating a synoptic gospel for each year makes the
basic structure of the three-year cycle easy to remember. It also fosters familiarity, for the readings recur every fourth year.

For all the variety that a three-year cycle of readings brings, there is
nonetheless a high degree of continuity from year to year. The same pattern of feasts, of festal seasons, and of Sundays in Ordinary Time is repeated every year, for the fundamental cycle of the liturgy is a yearly one
during which the most important facets of the mystery of Christ are celebrated. If over the three-year Lectionary cycle the readings change, the
same yearly calendar provides a stable, recurring structure.

Consonant with the annually-based liturgical calendar, the
Lectionary contributes to continuity by repeating important biblical pas-

---

[4]W. Skudlarek, *The Word in Worship*, 35.
[5]The total is not simply one year's readings multiplied by three, for a number of passages recur in each of the three years, e.g., the texts for Easter Sunday; most of the texts for
the Easter triduum; the gospel passage for the second Sunday of Easter, etc.

sages every year. To take examples from the gospels only, on sixteen of the sixty-nine annual Sunday and Feast Day Eucharists the *same* gospel passage is read in every year of the cycle. Furthermore, in a number of instances the *parallel stories* from the three synoptic gospels appear in each of their respective years, both in festal seasons and in ordinary time. In the festal season of Advent, for example, the Lectionary assigns the story of John the Baptist as the voice crying in the wilderness to the Third Sunday of every year. The Matthean version appears on the Third Sunday of Advent Year A, the Marcan version on the Third Sunday of Advent Year B, and the Lucan version on the Third Sunday of Advent Year C. Parallels from the synoptic gospels appear in their respective years for the Baptism of Jesus, the First and Second Sundays of Lent, Palm Sunday, and the Easter vigil.

The same phenomenon occurs on a number of Sundays in Ordinary Time as well. Certain gospel episodes are considered so important to the story of Jesus that the parallel episodes from each of the three synoptic gospels appear in their respective years. For example, the Matthean version of Peter's confession at Caesarea-Philippi that Jesus is the Christ occurs on the Twenty-first Sunday in Ordinary Time Year A, the Marcan version on the Twenty-fourth Sunday Year B, and the Lucan version on the Twelfth Sunday Year C. There are, finally, *thematic* parallels that appear in all three years, such as the call of the disciples, the mission of the seventy-two disciples, the announcement that the Kingdom is at hand, the warning to stay awake for the coming of the Son of Man. In this way the three-year-cycle Lectionary maintains a strong note of continuity within variety.

Three Readings for Each Sunday and Feast Day

The number of biblical passages that the revised Lectionary should assign to be read on each Sunday and Feast Day was another important question facing the committee. Research showed that in the long history of Christianity, different Churches had adopted a variety of practices. The Lectionary contained in the 1570 Roman Missal offered two readings only, both drawn from the New Testament (with Old Testament passages assigned on only three occasions). Different traditions reaching back to the fourth, fifth, and sixth centuries had three, four, five, even six readings at the Sunday Eucharist. Some Churches divided the New Testament into two categories (gospels and apostolic writings), others into three (gospels, Acts of the Apostles, apostolic writings). In some cases the entire Old Testament was considered as a unit, in other instances it was divided into two (the

Law and the rest), or three categories (the Law, Prophets, and Writings), with a reading selected from each. The committee settled on three readings per Sunday and Feast Day celebration, counting the Old Testament as one unit and dividing the New Testament into two categories (gospels and apostolic writings). They did so for the following reasons.

First, the fact that the Sunday liturgy culminates in the celebration of the Eucharist demands that a passage from one of the gospels be read. This constant practice in Christian Churches of all traditions reaches back to the earliest centuries. Second, a reading from one of the non-gospel books of the New Testament also represented a long-standing characteristic of Sunday celebrations, a tradition solidly preserved in the Lectionary of the 1570 Roman Missal. Although these books do not narrate the story of Jesus, they offer theological interpretations of his paschal mystery and examples of how the earliest communities of Christians actualized it in their lives. Given the nature of liturgy as *praxis*, and given the highly christocentric orientation of the Sunday Eucharist, it was deemed most appropriate to continue including passages from the apostolic writings in the revised Lectionary.

Third, the Constitution on the Sacred Liturgy strongly urged the reintroduction of Old Testament readings at the Eucharist, an ancient liturgical practice unfortunately abandoned as far back as the seventh century. Fourth- and fifth-century traditions all had at least one reading from the Old Testament at the Sunday Eucharist. Should the revised Lectionary return to the practice of some ancient Churches which had two or three readings from the Old Testament, followed by two or three readings from the New Testament? Here the demands and realities of modern life, where Sunday assemblies last at most one hour, made this idea impracticable. Should the reformed Lectionary keep the pre-Vatican II Lectionary's pattern of two readings per Sunday, substituting for the selections from the apostolic books passages from the Old Testament? But then the apostolic letters, which have always played such a prominent role in the history of church doctrine and of liturgical *praxis*, would never be heard by the Sunday assembly.

The committee felt it best to retain the tradition of two New Testament readings embedded in the Roman Missal of 1570 and to honor the council's wish by recovering the ancient tradition of a reading from the Old Testament. The Old Testament would be read first, followed by a passage from the apostolic writings, culminating with the gospel passage of the day. In this way each Sunday and Feast Day would find its focus in the paschal mystery—Jesus (the gospel passage) interpreted (the excerpt from the apostolic writing) as the fulfillment of salvation history (the Old Testament reading).

This is essentially what the 1981 Introduction to the *Lectionary for Mass* suggests when it states:

> Each Mass has three readings: the first from the Old Testament, the second from an apostle (that is, either from a letter or from Revelation, depending upon the season), and the third from the gospels. This arrangement brings out the unity of the Old and New Testaments and of the history of salvation, in which Christ is the central figure, commemorated in his paschal mystery (no. 66.1).

Mary Schaefer proposes a felicitous image which grasps the purpose of three readings at each Sunday and Feast Day eucharistic celebration: "By means similar to a geologist's extraction of a core sample, the Lectionary extracts a vertical core: Hebrew scriptures, apostolic letters and gospel pericopes, representing, in brief, the whole Judaeo-Christian story, biblical witness to revelation."[6] Thus, no matter what the specific content of a passage might be, each of the three readings on any given Sunday or Feast Day contributes an essential dimension to the celebration of the paschal mystery.

The Preeminence of the Gospel Reading

The gospel is the most important of the three readings. Two main factors contribute to the gospel's preeminence, one emanating from the nature of the gospels themselves, the other resulting from the liturgical context in which they are read.

First, the gospels are unique among the books of the New Testament in that they relate the story of Jesus' life, death, and resurrection: "It is evident that among all the inspired writings, even those of the new Testament, the gospels rightly have the supreme place, because they form the primary testimony to the life and teaching of the incarnate Word, our saviour" (Dogmatic Constitution on Divine Revelation [*Dei Verbum*], no. 18). This has led the Christian tradition to rank the gospels in a category separate from the other New Testament books: "Thus the liturgical traditions of both the East and the West have consistently continued to preserve some distinction between the books for the readings" (*ILM*, no. 36).

---

[6]Mary Schaefer, "Preaching: Word of God, Word of Ecclesial Faith," *Celebrate!* 32/4 (July-August 1993) 25.

Second, the Sunday Eucharist, because it is the ritual celebration of the paschal mystery and the actualization of Christ's presence, invites the proclamation of the Lord's words and deeds. The 1981 Introduction to the *Lectionary for Mass* elaborates: "The reading of the gospel is the high point of the liturgy of the word. For this the other readings, in their established sequence from the Old to the New Testament, prepare the assembly" (no. 13; cf. no. 36). The revised Lectionary continues this tradition which has perdured throughout the centuries.

The Lectionary manifests the preeminence of the gospels in the Sunday eucharistic liturgy in several ways. The gospel is proclaimed last, as the climax of the three readings. Consistent with ancient tradition, the gospel excerpt is constitutive of most of the major feasts of the liturgical year (e.g., the story of the birth of Jesus at Christmas, the discovery of the empty tomb at Easter, etc.). The gospel selections take precedence over the other readings in expressing the main themes of each festal season. As well, in these high liturgical moments and seasons the gospel passages provide images and phrases which are often woven into the fabric of collects, prefaces, and blessings, as made particularly evident in the new ICEL prayers. The gospel passage also plays a key role in Ordinary Time: on each Sunday, the gospel passage determines the selection of the accompanying first reading from the Old Testament.

Finally, the special prominence given to the gospel reading at the Sunday assembly has been expressed in a variety of ritual traditions, many dating back to the fourth and fifth centuries. For example, from the most ancient tradition to this day, only ordained ministers (bishops, priests, and deacons) proclaim the gospel. They also sign the book and themselves with the cross before, and kiss the gospel book after, reading. The assembly greets the gospel reading with a sung acclamation and stands during the proclamation. Only the gospel reading is introduced with "The Lord be with you" and its response. On occasion, the proclaiming of the gospel is solemnized by a procession with candles and incensing of the book. Finally, in earlier centuries when there were separate Lectionaries for gospels (evangelaries) and for epistles (epistolaries), the more ornate was the gospel book, a practice encouraged today: "In our times also, then, it is very desirable that cathedrals and at least the larger, more populous parishes and the churches with a larger attendance possess a beautifully designed Book of the Gospels, separate from the other book of readings" (*ILM,* no. 36). The gospels represent the presence of Christ. Thus the Church has always venerated the book of gospels as it venerates the Lord himself.

Because it has always enjoyed such pride of place, the gospel reading was the first of the three readings to be the object of the Lectionary reform committee's attention. Once the selection and distribution patterns for this reading were determined, the first and second readings more easily fell into place.

The First Reading: The Old Testament

Another hallmark of the revised Sunday and Feast Day Lectionary is the reintroduction, after a hiatus of more than a thousand years, of the Old Testament. Although the Constitution on the Sacred Liturgy contains no explicit mandate to do so, the scope of the document's paragraph 51 clearly intends the inclusion of the Old Testament:[7]

> In order that believers can be provided with a richer diet of God's word, the rich heritage of the Bible is to be opened more widely, in such a way that a fuller and more nourishing selection of the scriptures gets read to the people within a fixed period of years.

Accordingly, the revised Lectionary assigns an Old Testament passage as first reading on each Sunday and solemnity, except in the Easter Season.

By valuing the Old Testament to the point of including it as an essential part of the Sunday Eucharist, the Church manifests its faithfulness to Jesus. Jesus was a Jew. The scriptures of the people of Israel permeated his world and shaped his identity; the psalms nourished his prayer; the law and the prophets provided the images and motifs woven into the fabric of his preaching and teaching. It was these scriptures that he had been sent to fulfill.[8]

The Old Testament was the scripture of the first Christian generations. As evidenced on nearly every page of the New Testament, the authors of the gospels and of the apostolic writings turned again and again to the scriptures as the primary source from which to draw their interpretations of Jesus' death and resurrection. In doing so they followed the lead of the risen Christ himself who, ". . . beginning with Moses and all the prophets, interpreted to [the disciples of Emmaus] the things about himself in all the scriptures" (Luke 24:27). By including the Old Testament, the revised liturgy manifests its fidelity to the early Christian generations.

[7]Pierre Jounel, "Commentaire complet de la Constitution Conciliaire sur la liturgie," *La Maison-Dieu* 77 (1964) 120–1.

[8]Paul-Marie Guillaume, "Pourquoi une lecture de l'Ancien Testament?" *Assemblées du Seigneur* no. 3 (2e série; Paris: Cerf, 1964) 31–47.

In the first centuries of Christianity, the Old Testament featured highly in the voluminous homilies of the Church Fathers. In addition to finding Old Testament examples worthy of emulation, at every turn these Church leaders never tired of exploring the intimate link between the Old and New Testaments. The Vatican II Dogmatic Constitution on Divine Revelation recaptures this ancient appreciation of the Old Testament when it states:

> God, the inspirer and originator of the books of both testaments, has brought it about in his wisdom that the new Testament should be hidden in the old, and the old Testament should be made manifest in the new. Though Christ established the new covenant in his blood (see Lk 22:20; 1 Cor 11:25), nevertheless the old Testament books, all and entire, were retained in the preaching of the gospel; in the new Testament they acquire and display their full meaning (see Mt 5:17; Lk 24:27; Rm 16:25-26; 2 Cor 3:14-16), and in their turn they shed light on it and explain it (*DV*, no. 16).

By placing an Old Testament passage alongside New Testament excerpts, the Lectionary underscores the essential unity of the history of salvation. Only against the background of the entire sweep of Israel's history can the full significance of the paschal mystery be appreciated. For example, Christians can better appreciate the significance of the Eucharist when Paul's version of the Lord's supper is paired with the Passover prescriptions of Exodus 12 (Mass of the Lord's Supper, Years A, B, and C), or when Jesus' discourse on the bread of life has been preceded with the Exodus 16 story of manna in the desert (Eighteenth Sunday in Ordinary Time, Year B). Moreover, by evoking the history of Israel at the Sunday assembly, the Lectionary saves these stories from oblivion among Christians and helps them appropriate this history as their own. The Old Testament scriptures establish the foundation for the assembly's identity as the people of God.

In the revised Sunday Lectionary, the mutually enlightening relationship between the Old and New Testaments takes three basic forms: during Advent and Christmas, the Old Testament readings articulate the main themes of the season; during the Sundays of Lent they present an overview of salvation history; during the Sundays in Ordinary Time they correspond with the gospel passage of the day. The overall effect is that of a mosaic of the most important passages from the Old Testament, that, when viewed as a whole, adds breadth and depth to the Church's celebration of the paschal mystery.[9]

---

[9]Claude Wiéner, "L'Ancien Testament dans le lectionnaire dominical," *La Maison-Dieu* 166 (1986) 47–60.

The Second Reading: The Apostolic Writings

In continuity with the *Missale Romanum* of 1570, and faithful to ancient Roman tradition reaching back to the earliest Lectionaries, the revised Lectionary assigns a reading from the apostolic writings to each Sunday and Feast Day eucharistic celebration. Placing this excerpt between the Old Testament reading and the gospel reading is also in line with very ancient liturgical practice.[10]

The description of these biblical books sketched in the Dogmatic Constitution on Divine Revelation suggests why they so highly merit proclamation in the midst of the liturgical assembly:

> Besides the four gospels, the new Testament canon also contains the letters of Paul and other apostolic writings, which were also composed under the inspiration of the holy Spirit. By God's wise plan, these writings contain confirmation of what is told about Christ, give further explanation of his authentic teaching, preach about how Christ's divine work has power to save, tell the story of the church's beginnings and wonderful expansion, and foretell its glorious consummation (*DV*, no. 20).

The document first comments on the apostolic letters of Paul, Peter, James, Jude, and John. These books interpret the death and resurrection of Jesus in light of the scriptures, explore the full significance of the Christ event for believers and for all humankind, and proclaim God's saving deed for all to hear. They also exhort the faithful to live fully in Christ, both within their communities and in the greater social world to which they belong.

By the phrase "the story of the church's beginnings and wonderful expansion" the document brings to mind the Acts of the Apostles, Luke's narrative of the Church's birth and expansion from Jerusalem to Rome. Lastly, the constitution evokes the Book of Revelation. Its apocalyptic imagery expresses the goal of this earthly pilgrimage: God's final victory over the powers of sin and death, and the establishing of a new heavens and a new earth where God will reign forever. These New Testament books, then, point out the many ways the earliest Christians appropriated the paschal mystery in their lives. By offering passages from these writings, the Lectionary provides today's assemblies with the model and the sanction to continue doing the same.

---

[10]O. Rousseau, "Lecture et présence de l'Apôtre à la liturgie de la messe," *La Maison-Dieu* 62 (1960) 69–78.

In the Sunday and Feast Day Lectionary, the readings from the apostolic writings are distributed according to two fundamental patterns. For feasts and festal seasons, the passages reflect the main theme being celebrated, and often serve as a bridge between the first and third readings; for the Sundays in Ordinary Time, semicontinuous sequences of passages, read over several successive Sundays, offer a more substantial presentation of the letters of Paul, the Letter of James, and the Letter to the Hebrews.

Principles of Reading Selection and Distribution

The liturgical year consists of two types of seasons, festal seasons (Advent, Christmas, Lent, and Easter), and Ordinary Time. The Sunday and Feast Day Lectionary reflects this distinction by employing different principles of selecting and distributing readings for each kind of season. Although selecting and distributing passages are two different activities, the principles underlying them are so closely interwoven that it is best to treat them as one topic.

As the overall distinctive mark of the festal seasons, the Lectionary employs *lectio selecta*, readings selected to articulate the season or feast being celebrated. *Lectio selecta* appears in three modalities: harmony, thematic groupings, and correspondence. As the general distinctive mark of the Sundays in Ordinary Time, the Lectionary uses semicontinuous reading. This is a modern adaption of the ancient practice of *lectio continua*, the sequential reading of entire biblical books over a determined number of successive Sundays. Semicontinuous reading consists of a sequential reading, not of an entire book, but of *selected* passages from a book.

Lectio continua affirms that all of scripture is the Word of God and intended for instruction. It is the oldest principle of reading selection and distribution in Christian liturgy, dating back to the earliest centuries of the Church before the development of festal seasons. *Lectio selecta*, which evolved along with the festal seasons, underscores the significance of the present event being celebrated and its importance in the ongoing history of salvation.[11] By employing these two key principles, the revised Lectionary maintains continuity with the earliest liturgical practice of the Church.

Of the three modalities of *lectio selecta* characterizing the festal seasons, the most important is harmony. Harmony consists in the selection of biblical books or biblical passages in light of their aptness to express the

---

[11] Pierre Jounel, "La Bible dans la liturgie," in *Parole de Dieu et Liturgie* (*Lex Orandi* 25; Paris: Cerf, 1958) 24.

main themes of a season or a feast. In most cases ancient Christian tradition has already designated such texts, for example, the reading of Acts of the Apostles and Revelation during Eastertide, Isaiah during Advent, Matthew's and Luke's stories of Jesus' infancy at Christmas, etc. The Lectionary then arranges the selected passages in three types of patterns: thematic groupings, correspondence, and semicontinuous reading.

Through thematic groupings the Lectionary shapes and structures a liturgical season by fleshing out its fundamental themes. For example, besides preparing for Christmas, Advent also looks forward to Christ's second coming at the end of time. To articulate this characteristic Advent theme, all three readings for the first and second Sundays of Advent, across all three Lectionary years A, B, and C, are replete with eschatological images. In a similar fashion, thematic groupings are present in Lent, the season of preparation for Easter. In Year A the gospels for the Third, Fourth, and Fifth Sundays of Lent focus their attention on the catechumens who will be initiated in the faith at the Easter vigil. In Year B the gospels for the same three Sundays underline Jesus' journey through death to new life. In Year C the gospels for those three Sundays stress penance and conversion. Still other thematic groupings can be discerned in the Sundays of Easter and in the Christmas season. Thematic groupings, then, contribute an essential dimension to the Lectionary's architecture.

The next modality of *lectio selecta* is correspondence. This term refers to the intentional link between two or among three readings of a eucharistic celebration. Although the 1981 Introduction to the *Lectionary for Mass* calls this relationship between readings "harmony of another kind" (no. 67), it is perhaps better to reserve the word "harmony" for the selecting of biblical books and passages that articulate the themes of the season or feast day and to use the term "correspondence" to describe the narrower link among the readings of a given celebration. Correspondence is pervasive in festal seasons and solemnities, for by their nature these high liturgical moments demand a greater unity among the prescribed readings. A good example of correspondence occurs on the First Sunday of Lent Year A. The Old Testament reading relates the story of the temptation and fall of Adam and Eve from Genesis 2–3. The excerpt corresponds with the gospel of the day, Matthew 4:1-11, where Jesus is also tempted by Satan but does not succumb as did Adam and Eve; the second reading, drawn from Romans 5:12-19, links the first and third readings with Paul's typological comparison of Adam and Christ, the last Adam.

In addition to harmony, thematic groupings, and correspondence, the Lectionary also employs semicontinuous reading during the festal season of Easter. The second readings from the apostolic writings for all three Lectionary years (1 Peter in Year A, 1 John in Year B, and Revelation in Year C) are distributed according to this pattern. Finally, a slightly adapted form of semicontinuous distribution structures the first readings from Acts of the Apostles.

Semicontinuous reading characterizes the Sundays in Ordinary Time. This distribution pattern applies to the gospel readings and to the readings from the apostolic letters, each of which follows its own independent sequence. As a result, only rarely is there correspondence between the second and third readings on any given Sunday. The Old Testament reading, however, in most instances corresponds with the gospel passage of the day.

The members of *Coetus XI* deliberately chose this arrangement. They could easily enough have selected both the Old Testament reading and the reading from the apostolic letters to correspond with the gospel passage of the day. The 1981 Introduction to the *Lectionary for Mass* explains why they chose not to do so:

> The decision was made not to extend to Sundays the arrangement suited to the liturgical seasons mentioned [Lent-Easter, Advent-Christmas], that is, not to have an organic harmony of themes designed to aid homiletic instruction. Such an arrangement would be in conflict with the genuine conception of liturgical celebration. The liturgy is always the celebration of the mystery of Christ and makes use of the word of God on the basis of its own tradition, guided not by merely logical concerns but by the desire to proclaim the Gospel and to lead those who believe to the fullness of truth (no. 68).

The distribution of readings characteristic of Ordinary Time reminds the Church that every eucharistic celebration is always and above all a celebration of the paschal mystery of Christ. In each instance the Old Testament passage evokes the history of salvation of which Jesus, presented in the gospel excerpt, is the center and fulfillment, interpreted and appropriated by the Christian community as modeled in the apostolic writings. In this way the Lectionary's principles of reading selection and patterns of reading distribution serve the liturgy, whose aim is to configure the worshipping assembly into the paschal mystery of Jesus Christ.

Length of Readings

The addition of a third reading on each Sunday and solemnity to the traditional two readings of the 1570 Roman Missal necessarily lengthened the Liturgy of the Word.[12] Setting aside the longer passages (such as the Passion narratives and the three chapters from John's gospel read in Lent Year A), the average length of the gospel reading in the revised Sunday Lectionary tabulates to 10.5 verses (9.2 verses in the 1570 Roman Missal). The average length of the second reading from the apostolic writings is 5.8 verses (7.6 verses in the 1570 Roman Missal). Setting aside the longer readings for the Easter Triduum and Pentecost Vigil, the average length of the Old Testament reading is 5.5 verses (the 1570 Roman Missal had no Sunday Old Testament readings). The average length of the readings from Acts of the Apostles, which replace the Old Testament during the Easter season, comes to 8.2 verses. To compensate for the added length, the second readings for this season have been shortened. In total, the average length of the Liturgy of the Word in the new Lectionary is 21.8 verses (16.8 verses in the Roman Missal of 1570).

The Proportion of the Bible in the Sunday and Feast Day Lectionary

The revised Sunday and Feast Day Lectionary, with its three readings per eucharistic celebration distributed over a three-year cycle, more than triples the number of biblical passages contained in its predecessor, the *Missale Romanum* of 1570. How much of the entire Bible does this *praestantior pars* of scripture represent?

Catholics recognize forty-five books as constituting the Old Testament. Thirty-two of these books are represented in the revised Sunday Lectionary; thirteen do not appear at all (Judges, Ruth, 1 Chronicles, Ezra, Esther, Song of Songs, Lamentations, Obadiah, Nahum, Haggai, Tobit, Judith, 1 Maccabees). The forty-five Old Testament books contain some 27,300 verses, from which a total of about 1,550 verses are selected, distributed in 164 pericopes.[13] This tallies to 5.7 percent of the Old Testament. The Book of the Prophet Isaiah is the most cited (172 of its 1,292 verses, or 13.3 percent), followed by Exodus (115 of 1,211 verses, or 9.5 percent), then Genesis (141 of 1,562 verses, or 9 percent).

The New Testament is much shorter than the Old Testament, but it is much more extensively employed. Together the twenty-seven New Testament books, of which twenty-four are represented (only the Second and Third Letters of John and the Letter of Jude do not appear at all), con-

---

[12]The statistics presented here are drawn from E. Nübold, *Entstehung*, 192–3, 282, 334–5.

[13]The statistics in this section are tabulated on the New Revised Standard Version.

tain a total of 7,969 verses. Of these, 3,294 verses (or 41.3 percent) appear in the Sunday and Feast Day Lectionary, distributed in 388 passages (185 gospel pericopes, 203 from the apostolic writings). As expected, the books most often quoted are the four gospels: 57.1 percent of Matthew appears in the Lectionary, 61.4 percent of Mark, 58.2 percent of Luke, and 61 percent of John. It is worth noting that even though John's gospel does not have its own year, it is nevertheless as amply used as the three synoptic gospels. After the gospels, the most quoted books are Acts of the Apostles and Paul's letters to the Romans and First Corinthians, followed by Ephesians and Hebrews. In comparison, the 1570 Lectionary contained 1,253 (15.8 percent) of the 7,969 verses in the New Testament and only 261 (1 percent) of the 24,837 verses in the Old Testament, not counting the Psalms. In all it included 1,514 of the 32,852 verses in the Bible (4.6 percent), excluding the Psalms.

These statistics show that, according to the Lectionary reform committee and the scholars it consulted, the essential part (*praestantior pars*) of scripture, both Old and New Testaments, tallies to about 13.7 percent of the whole. The Sunday and Feast Day Lectionary indeed offers a richer fare at the table of God's word by presenting a much wider selection of readings than did the 1570 Roman Missal. Nevertheless, the Lectionary still presents under one-sixth of the Bible in a three-year cycle of readings.

Two implications can be drawn from these statistics. First, the Lectionary offers a (liturgical) canon within a canon. It is a "liturgical Bible," or more precisely still, a "Sunday eucharistic Bible." What the Sunday assembly hears of the scriptures is what both tradition and Vatican II propose as the most important passages. Second, that the Lectionary contains such a small fraction of the whole Bible implies that the Sunday Eucharist cannot pretend to be the first and foremost occasion for the faithful to be exposed to and become familiar with the scriptures. The Lectionary presupposes an adequate acquaintance with the Bible. It serves an anamnetic purpose, to recall and evoke the key moments and reflections of the history of salvation centered in the paschal mystery.

Determining What Constitutes a Reading

A Lectionary presents an ordered *selection* of biblical passages for liturgical proclamation. What criteria did the members of *Coetus XI* employ in determining what constitutes a reading for the Sunday and Feast Day Lectionary? The 1981 Introduction to the *Lectionary for Mass* lists four: (1.) Reservation of some books on the basis of the liturgical seasons, (2.) Length of texts, (3.) Difficult texts, (4.) Omission of texts (*ILM*, nos. 73–77).

1. The first criterion has been dealt with above under the heading *Principles of Reading Selection and Distribution*.

2. The second criterion has been partially dealt with under the heading *Length of Readings*, but here it merits further elaboration. First, exegetical considerations based on an examination of literary genres and forms influenced the length of a reading, as noted in the 1981 Introduction: "A distinction has been made between narratives, which require reading a fairly long passage but which usually hold people's attention, and texts that should not be lengthy because of the profundity of their teaching" (no. 75). Second, in about forty cases, where the selected narrative passage is significantly longer than average, the Lectionary offers a choice between a longer and a shorter reading "to suit different situations" (*ILM*, no. 75).

3. The third criterion concerns difficult texts. The 1981 Introduction explains:

> In readings for Sundays and solemnities, texts that present real difficulties are avoided for pastoral reasons. The difficulties may be objective, in that the texts themselves raise complex literary, critical, or exegetical problems; or, at least to a certain extent, the difficulties may lie in the faithful's ability to understand the texts . . . (no. 76).

Not every passage in the Bible is suitable for liturgical proclamation. The ancient Jewish synagogue eschewed certain texts in its worship, such as the violent episodes in the Book of Judges and the mystical opening chapters of the prophet Ezekiel. In Christian tradition, passages like the lengthy legal prescriptions in Leviticus, as important as they are for understanding the history and religion of the people of Israel, have no direct bearing in Christian life and are therefore deemed unsuitable for liturgical proclamation. In both Jewish and Christian traditions, the context of worship and prayer determines what scriptural passages are to be read. Nevertheless, the mere fact that a text is difficult did not necessarily lead to its exclusion from the revised Lectionary, as the 1981 Introduction to the *Lectionary for Mass* both cautions and admonishes:

> But there could be no justification for depriving the faithful of the spiritual riches of certain texts on the grounds of difficulty if its source is the inadequacy either of the religious education that every Christian should have or of the biblical formation that every pastor should have (no. 76).

4. The last criterion concerns the omission of verses. On this topic the 1981 Introduction states:

> The omission of verses in readings from Scripture has at times been the practice in many liturgical traditions, including the Roman. Admittedly such omissions may not be made lightly, for fear of distorting the meaning of the text or the intent and style of Scripture (*ILM*, no. 77).

The revisers of the Sunday Lectionary engaged in this practice quite extensively. Omission of verses occurs most often in Old Testament readings, less so in selections from the apostolic writings, and least of all in gospel pericopes. There are two main reasons for omitting verses:

> One reason for the decision is that otherwise some texts would have been unduly long. It would also have been necessary to omit completely certain readings of high spiritual value for the faithful because those readings include some verse that is unsuitable pastorally or that involves truly difficult problems (no. 77).

Thus length and unsuitability play an important role in the decision to exclude verses. Omission of verses can take a variety of forms. Eileen Schuller notes six general patterns: (a) stage directions (information about the setting, characters, etc., not essential to the passage); (b) names of people and places (information often not useful in liturgical contexts); (c) non-essential information (e.g., etymologies of Old Testament names); (d) harsh verses (e.g., verses containing violence); (e) omission of the unseemly (e.g., descriptions of bodily, especially sexual, parts and functions); (f) omission to highlight the link with the gospel (verses in the first or second reading that would contradict or deflect the orientation of the gospel pericope).[14]

Both the omission of difficult texts and the omission of verses entail a certain amount of subjectivity—what is difficult or unsuitable to one person is not necessarily so to another. Adjustments on the scale of individual verses can easily enough be made in successive editions. The 1981 edition of the Sunday Lectionary, for example, has introduced twelve such changes to the 1969 edition. There is every reason to believe that, for pastoral reasons based on comments from worshippers the world over, changes on the scale of entire passages or sections of passages will also be implemented in later editions.

---

[14]Eileen Schuller, "Some Criteria for the Choice of Scripture Texts in the Roman Lectionary," *Shaping English Liturgy: Studies in Honor of Archbishop Denis Hurley*, eds. Peter C. Finn and James M. Schelman (Washington, D.C.: The Pastoral Press, 1990) 385–404, especially 395–400.

The Ecumenical Import of the Sunday and Feast Day Lectionary[15]

The 1969 publication of the *Lectionary for Mass* unexpectedly launched an unprecedented ecumenical rapprochement on the use of the Bible in worship. Within a decade of its appearance, a number of Churches in North America adopted the Roman Catholic Sunday Lectionary, and adapted it where necessary to meet the worship needs of their congregations.[16] Since this resulted in five slightly different variations of the Sunday Lectionary, interested Churches sought agreement on a standard edition. The already-existing Consultation on Common Texts[17] took the initiative and in 1978 gathered representatives of thirteen Churches from Canada and the United States to study the situation. The participants concurred on the value of the Roman Catholic Sunday Lectionary as the basis for a common lectionary, and formed a working group called the North American Committee on Calendar and Lectionary (NACCL) to pursue a standardized adaptation. In 1983, the group published a proposed *Common Lectionary* and formed a Lectionary Task Force to collect suggestions and responses from the participating Churches that used it for worship. This led to the *Revised Common Lectionary* published in 1992.[18]

The Roman Catholic Sunday Lectionary and the *Revised Common Lectionary* share the following features:

---

[15] The section contains slightly revised material from my article "Sharing at the Table of the Word: The Sunday Lectionary" that appeared in *Ecumenism* 31/122 (June 1996) 21-3.

[16] The Presbyterian Churches in the United States (1970), the Episcopal Church (1970), the Lutheran Church in the United States (1970), a consensus edition published by the ecumenical Consultation on Church Union representing nine Protestant Churches (1974), the Methodist Church in the United States (1976), the Disciples of Christ (who adopted the Presbyterian edition in 1976). In Canada, both the United Church and the Anglican Church first adopted and adapted the Roman Catholic Sunday Lectionary in 1980.

[17] The CCT was a result of Vatican II's decision to implement the vernacular. This led a number of Protestant Church leaders to initiate overtures to North American Roman Catholic authorities toward the formulation of common liturgical texts. The first gathering included representatives from the Inter-Lutheran Commission on Worship, the Protestant Episcopal Church, the United Presbyterian Church, the Worship Commission of the Consultation on Church Union (COCU), and the International Commission on English in the Liturgy (ICEL) of the Roman Catholic Church. See Horace T. Allen, Jr., "Consultation on Common Texts," *New Catholic Encyclopedia* vol. 17 (Washington, D.C.; New York: McGraw-Hill, 1967) 153–4.

[18] Consultation on Common Texts, *Common Lectionary: The Lectionary Proposed by the Consultation on Common Texts* (New York: The Church Hymnal Corp., 1983); Ibid., *The Revised Common Lectionary* (Nashville: Abingdon, 1992).

- The same annual calendar, with the Lord's Day as the fundamental Christian feast, plus the festal seasons of Advent-Christmas and Lent-Easter

- The same three-year cycle of readings, Matthew's gospel assigned to Year A, Mark's to Year B, and Luke's to Year C (John's gospel appears in Lent and Easter, and supplements Mark's in Year B), with nearly unanimous agreement on gospel selections throughout the cycle

- Three readings per Sunday, the first from the Hebrew scriptures (except during Easter, where the first reading is drawn from the Acts of the Apostles), the second from the apostolic writings, and the third from the gospels. A responsorial psalm follows the proclamation of the first reading.

Differences occur in the selections from the apostolic writings, which in the *Revised Common Lectionary* have often been lengthened. There are more substantive differences between the two Lectionaries in the first reading from the Hebrew scriptures. Because the designers of the *Common Lectionary* were concerned about the Roman Catholic Sunday Lectionary's strict "typological" choice of Old Testament pericopes, they

> . . . proposed a revision of the Roman table for a number of Sundays of the year in each of the three [years of the cycle]. The lessons are still typologically controlled by the Gospel, but in a broader way than Sunday by Sunday, in order to make possible semicontinuous reading of some significant Old Testament narratives.[19]

The 1992 *Revised Common Lectionary* goes yet a step further in the adaptation of the Old Testament first readings. To meet the needs both of Churches that celebrate the Eucharist every Sunday and of Churches that celebrate Eucharist monthly or quarterly, the *Revised Common Lectionary* offers two tracks for the first reading. One follows the Roman Catholic Sunday Lectionary in providing an Old Testament selection consonant with the gospel passage of the day; the other favors a semicontinuous reading of more extensive narrative sequences for a number of Sundays of the year [Sundays in Ordinary Time]. In Year A, paired with Matthew's gospel is "a semicontinuous series of readings that focus on the major Genesis narratives, the covenant with Moses, and the establishment of

---

[19] Horace T. Allen, Jr., "*Common Lectionary*: Origins, Assumptions, and Issues," *Studia Liturgica* 21 (1991) 17–8.

Israel in the promised land"; in Year B, "a series of semicontinuous readings that focus on the Davidic covenant and Wisdom literature" is read along with Mark's gospel; in Year C, the semicontinuous reading of Luke's gospel is accompanied by "a series of semicontinuous readings of the prophetic proclamation, chosen in chronological order and highlighting Jeremiah."[20] Overall, the similarities outweigh the differences, thus contributing to the great impetus in ecumenical sharing.

There is every reason to hope that the following ecumenical gains among those Churches using a three-year Sunday Lectionary will continue to develop:

- A renewed understanding of the balance of Word and Sacrament. If in the past Catholics stressed sacrament (Eucharist every Sunday and every weekday) and Reformed Churches emphasized the Word (Sunday Eucharist in a monthly or quarterly rhythm), now Catholics see that the Word provides the "why" of sacrament and Reformed Churches recognize that the Word must be "enfleshed" in Sacrament.[21] This necessarily leads to a better ecclesiology (the Church is what it says *and* does), stemming from a renewed appreciation of the centrality of the Mystery of Christ.
- A renewed appreciation of preaching as a biblically-based liturgical act of proclamation. The Bible is not merely a source of material mined to illustrate a preacher's ideas, but the story of God's saving actions proclaimed as real and effective today. Use of a Lectionary provides a solid basis for sustained biblical, liturgical preaching.[22]
- Collaboration among pastors and ministers in preparing homilies and liturgical celebrations. Use of the *Revised Common Lectionary* and the Roman Catholic Sunday Lectionary allows pastors from different Churches and communions to prepare celebrations and homilies together. The publication of liturgical and preaching aids

[20] Consultation on Common Texts, *The Revised Common Lectionary* (Nashville: Abingdon, 1992) 16–7.

[21] Horace T. Allen, Jr., "The Ecumenical Import of Lectionary Reform," *Shaping English Liturgy*, 376–7.

[22] Keith Watkins, "Protestants Rediscover the Word?" *Worship* 53 (1979) 119–25; Peter C. Bower, "Introduction," *Handbook for the Common Lectionary*, Peter C. Bower, ed., (Philadelphia: The Geneva Press, 1987) 15–40; Fred B. Anderson, "Protestant Worship Today," *Theology Today* 43 (1986) 65–7.

based on these two Lectionaries further encourages sharing across denominational lines.[23]

The promulgation of the Roman Catholic Sunday Lectionary and the enthusiastic adoption of the *Revised Common Lectionary* bode well for ecumenism. The more different Churches and congregations share at the "table of God's word" by using common scriptural passages for proclamation and preaching, the more they will realize that indeed they are united in "one Lord, one faith, one baptism, one God and Father of all" (Eph 4:5-6).

Conclusion

The Vatican II Sunday and Feast Day Lectionary is the result of the most informed and thorough Lectionary revision ever carried out in the Church's history. Far from being an arbitrary assemblage of disjointed biblical passages, it is rather a carefully constructed whole articulated on the basis of liturgical principles and pastoral concerns. Hence it is important to study it with its architecture, as much as the contents of its individual biblical passages, in mind. To such a study is the second part of this book devoted.

[23]For example, *Proclamation* series published by Fortress Press; *Homily Service: An Ecumenical Resource for Sharing the Word* published by The Liturgical Conference; *Preaching the New Common Lectionary* by Abingdon.

PART TWO

ARCHITECTURE OF
THE SUNDAY AND FEAST DAY
LECTIONARY

Introduction

Part One surveyed the history of lectionaries, described the Vatican II reform of the Lectionary, and sketched the principal features of the current Sunday and Feast Day Lectionary. Part Two studies the patterns of reading selection and distribution in the Sunday Lectionary—its "architecture." The following chapters all proceed in three steps: (1) based on the *General Norms for the Liturgical Year and the Calendar* (*GNLYC*), a succinct description of a liturgical season and how it expresses the paschal mystery; (2) an overview of the principles of reading selection and distribution employed in that season; and (3) a detailed examination of the patterns or architecture of the scriptural readings structuring the liturgical season. Each of these steps requires further elaboration.

(1) *Centrality of the Paschal Mystery*. The Sunday and Feast Day Lectionary does not exist in isolation. It is part of the greater reality of Sunday and Feast Day eucharistic worship, which itself is organized in a yearly cycle. The Lectionary fleshes out the seasons, Sundays, and feasts of the liturgical year by assigning pertinent biblical passages to each. It is impossible to understand the rationale behind the Lectionary reading selection and distribution without an adequate grasp of the liturgical year, its seasons and feasts. The *GNLYC* provides just this needed information.[1] The product of *Coetus I* of the Vatican II *Consilium* on Liturgy, this document contains the descriptions of the liturgical days and liturgical seasons, as well as of the calendar on which the Eucharist and the Liturgy of the Hours are celebrated. The members of this important committee, like those of *Coetus XI* on the reform of the Lectionary, found their mandate for the revision of the liturgical calendar in the Constitution on the Sacred Liturgy:

[1] The full text of the document can be found in Elizabeth Hoffman, ed., *The Liturgy Documents: A Parish Resource*, Third Edition (Chicago: Liturgy Training Publications, 1991) 173–84.

The liturgical year is to be revised. The traditional customs and practices of the liturgical seasons are to be preserved or restored, in line with the circumstances of our time. Their basic thrust is to be retained, so that they nourish as they should people's religious observance in celebrating the mysteries of christian redemption—above all the easter mystery (*SC*, no. 107).

"And above all the easter [or paschal] mystery." These words contain the key to the revision not only of the Lectionary but of the liturgy as a whole. True to the council's encouragement to return to the sources of the liturgy, the members of *Coetus I* oriented the calendar more clearly to the central mystery of faith—Jesus' *passing over* from death to life (hence, *paschal,* an adjective derived from the Hebrew word for passover, *pascha*). Indeed, in his *motu proprio* of May 9, 1969, the allocution by which he officially promulgated the revised calendar, Pope Paul VI pressed home this point when he wrote:

> We are clearly instructed by the Second Vatican Council that the celebration of the Paschal Mystery is of the greatest importance in Christian liturgical worship, and that it unfolds throughout the course of days, weeks, and the whole year. From this it follows that the Paschal Mystery should receive greater prominence in the revision of the liturgical calendar (*Mysterii Paschalis Celebrationem*).[2]

The Lectionary, through its selection and distribution of scriptural readings, articulates the particular way each liturgical season relates to the paschal mystery. It puts biblical flesh on the skeleton of the calendar. There no doubt is a certain chronological sequence to the liturgical year, as the Constitution on the Sacred Liturgy points out: "Moreover, the church unfolds the whole mystery of Christ over the cycle of the year, from his incarnation and birth to this return to heaven, to the day of Pentecost, and to our waiting for our hope of bliss and the return of the Lord" (*SC*, no. 102). Nevertheless, the procedure adopted here intends to stress the *unfolding* of the mystery rather than its more biographically-based dimension. Hence, Part Two examines the Proper of Seasons in the sequence presented in the *GNLYC*, that is, moving from the center outward as the different seasons unfold the paschal mystery: the Easter Triduum, the Easter Season, Lent, Christmas, Advent, and Ordinary Time.

---

[2]As quoted in John H. Fitzsimmons, *Guide to the Lectionary* (Essex, England: Mayhew-McCrimmon, 1981) 22.

Indeed, this is the historical sequence in which the festal seasons which make up the liturgical year evolved.

(2) *The role of principles of reading selection and distribution in shaping the Lectionary*. The Lectionary employs the several principles of reading selection and distribution (discussed in chapter 3 above) in varying combinations depending on the liturgical season. This is done in part to remain true to ancient tradition, in part to give renewed prominence to the way each liturgical season relates to the paschal mystery. Each principle of reading selection and distribution itself contributes to the intricate structure of the liturgical year's celebration of the paschal mystery. For example, the principle of harmony helps select those biblical passages that best provide the themes, images, and language needed to celebrate those aspects of the paschal mystery highlighted in a particular season. The principle of correspondence, by which the readings of a eucharistic celebration are linked to one another, suggests the unity of the paschal mystery from its first foreshadowings in the Old Testament to its anticipated fulfillment in the Age to Come. Since the principles of reading selection and distribution play such an important role in the design of a liturgical season's Lectionary offerings, each of the following chapters offers an overview of the particular use a liturgical season makes of them.

(3) *Sunday—the original Christian feast*. Liturgical seasons, with the exception of Christmas, are made up of batches of Sundays. This comes as no surprise, for, as the Constitution on the Sacred Liturgy explains, Sunday is the original Christian feast:

> Every seventh day, the church celebrates the easter mystery. This is a tradition going back to the apostles, taking its origin from the actual day of Christ's resurrection—a day thus appropriately designated "the Lord's day." For on this day, christian believers should come together, in order to commemorate the suffering, resurrection and glory of the lord Jesus, by hearing God's word and sharing the Eucharist; and to give thanks to God who has made them, "born anew to a living hope through the resurrection of Jesus Christ from the dead" (1 Pet 1:3) (*SC*, no. 106).

At each Sunday Eucharist the Church celebrates the paschal mystery. But that is not all. Because it always was and remains the quintessential time to celebrate this central mystery of faith, Sunday "is the basis and center of the whole liturgical year" (*SC,* no. 106). The liturgical seasons which make up the liturgical year developed, historically and theologically, from the Sunday celebration of the paschal mystery. As the unfolding of Sunday, the liturgical seasons necessarily also flow out of and point to the paschal mystery. The themes of a liturgical season are not meant to overwhelm, but rather to enhance, the Sunday celebration of the paschal mystery. The Sundays in Lent, for example, celebrate the death *and resurrection* of Jesus—that is why the Sundays in Lent are not penitential (e.g., no penitential practices such as fasting). No matter the liturgical season in which they are found, Sundays always radiate the fundamental mystery of Christian faith.

The bulk of each chapter in Part Two, therefore, examines the patterns of scriptural readings across the Sundays and Feast Days of a liturgical season. These patterns provide an insight into what is perhaps the most important, influential, and far-reaching way the liturgy appropriates and interprets the scriptures.

4   The Easter Triduum[1]

The *General Norms for the Liturgical Year and the Calendar* (*GNLYC*) describes the Easter triduum in this way:

> Christ redeemed us all and gave perfect glory to God principally through his paschal mystery: dying he destroyed our death and rising he restored our life. Therefore the Easter triduum of the passion and resurrection of Christ is the culmination of the entire liturgical year. Thus the solemnity of Easter has the same kind of preeminence in the liturgical year that Sunday has in the week (no. 18).

> The Easter triduum begins with the evening Mass of the Lord's Supper, reaches its high point in the Easter vigil, and closes with evening prayer on Easter Sunday (no. 19).

Triduum, which comes from Latin for "three days," echoes the gospel phrase proclaiming Jesus' resurrection "on the third day." When qualified by the word "Easter," it refers to the one feast of the paschal mystery celebrated over a period of three days. The calculation of three days derives from the liturgy's way of reckoning time according to ancient Jewish tradition and still current in New Testament times: a day was measured from sundown to sundown. The first day of the triduum begins at the evening celebration of the Lord's Supper on Thursday and, because it extends to sundown on Friday, includes the celebration of the Lord's passion; the second day begins at sundown on Friday and ends at sundown on Saturday; the third day, from sundown on Saturday through to Sunday evening, reaches its high point in the vigil.

The Easter triduum marks the bridge between the season of Lent and the season of Easter. While the forty days of Lent evoke the pilgrim nature of the Church and the fifty days of Easter offer a foretaste of the promised

---

[1]Most of the material in this chapter is a revised version of my article on the Easter triduum that appeared in *Celebrate!* 34/2 (March–April 1995) 41–8.

glory awaiting us, the triduum paces believers from one to the other by celebrating the heart of the paschal mystery itself—Jesus' *passing over* from death to life, his *transitus* from this world to the Father. This it does through the ritual commemoration of his last hours, his crucifixion, his burial, and his resurrection on the third day.

Principles of Reading Selection and Distribution

For these most holy days, the Lectionary proposes the choicest readings from the scriptures according to the general principle of *lectio selecta*. This principle, characteristic of the Lectionary's way of dealing with feasts and festal seasons, appears in three modalities: harmony, thematic groupings, and correspondence. All three are employed for the triduum. First, the biblical excerpts deemed most apt, in light of ancient practice as well as of modern scholarship, to express the meaning of the feasts being celebrated have been selected. For example, John's gospel, traditionally read during Lent and Easter, naturally provides the gospels for Thursday, Friday, and Easter morning of the triduum, while key passages from Exodus are featured at the Mass of the Lord's Supper and at the vigil. Second, although not precisely in the sense found in Advent, Lent, and Easter, the readings of the triduum together contain such an interweaving of threads and an interplay of images that in effect they form one thematically unified tapestry. Finally, given that these feasts require such a highly select repertoire of biblical passages, there is a particularly strong accent placed on correspondence among the readings for each celebration, moreso than at any other time in the liturgical year (except perhaps Christmas and Epiphany).

Resurrection of the Lord—Easter Vigil (During the Night)

The following descriptions of the Easter vigil provided by the *GNLYC* suggests why it is preferable to begin the detailed study of the triduum here rather than with the Thursday Mass of the Lord's Supper:

> The Easter triduum begins with the evening Mass of the Lord's Supper, *reaches its high point in the Easter Vigil*, and closes with evening prayer on Easter Sunday.

> The Easter Vigil, during the holy night when Christ rose from the dead, *ranks as the "mother of all vigils"* [quoting Augustine, *Sermo* 219; PL 38, 1088]. Keeping watch, the Church awaits Christ's resurrection and celebrates it in the sacraments (nos. 19 and 21; emphases added).

In the early centuries of the Church, the vigil, as the name itself implies, lasted from after sundown on Saturday until dawn on Sunday. During this time of watching and waiting, the assembled community had the leisure to read all of Genesis and Exodus, as well as large segments of other biblical books, particularly the prophets. Thus the oldest and most fundamental part of the Easter vigil remains the Liturgy of the Word.[2] Near the end of the vigil, before dawn, the Christian community initiated its new members into the paschal mystery of Christ through the ritual of baptism. Finally, the assembly broke its three-day-long fast by celebrating the Eucharist at dawn on Easter morning, with the newly-baptized sharing for the first time at the table of the Lord. Due to a variety of historical contingencies, over the centuries this most solemn of feasts became progressively marginalized to the point where in the Tridentine liturgy the vigil was actually celebrated early Holy Saturday morning with virtually no one attending. The liturgical reforms under Pope Pius XII in the 1950s restored the vigil to its rightful place after sundown on Holy Saturday; the renewal of Vatican II simplified this liturgy and rightly reinstated it as the high point of the liturgical year. While the triduum is the culmination of the liturgical year, the vigil itself stands out as the high point of the triduum. The current prominence the Easter vigil now enjoys is one of the most important fruits of this century's liturgical research and reform.

The Lectionary assigns the following scriptural readings to the Easter vigil:

Old Testament:	Genesis 1:1–2:2*
	Genesis 22:1-18*
	Exodus 14:15–15:1*
	Isaiah 54:5-14
	Isaiah 55:1-11*
	Baruch 3:9-15, 32–4:4*
	Ezekiel 36:16-28
Apostolic Writings:	Romans 6:3-11
Gospel:	Year A: Matthew 28:1-10*
	Year B: Mark 16:1-8**
	Year C: Luke 24:1-12

* readings retained from *MR* 1570
** read on Easter Sunday in *MR* 1570

---

[2] Roger Greenacre and Jeremy Haselock, *The Sacrament of Easter* (Leominster, England: Fowler Wright Books, 1989) 132.

Far from the original sundown-to-dawn experience of the post-Constantinian Church, the current vigil lasts but a few hours at most. Instead of a continued reading from the Scriptures, especially the Old Testament, throughout the night, now the vigil offers only a distillation of the key moments in the story of salvation. Even with this highly-condensed ritual, there is nevertheless a temptation to shorten the Liturgy of the Word by not reading all nine of the prescribed passages, a practice permitted in most dioceses for pastoral reasons. Since the Liturgy of the Word is the most ancient and essential feature of the Easter vigil, however, in its circular letter *Preparing and Celebrating the Paschal Feasts* the Congregation for Divine Worship urges that "wherever this is possible, all the readings should be read so that the character of the Easter Vigil, which demands it should be somewhat prolonged, be respected at all costs" (no. 85).[3]

There is an order of priority among the Old Testament readings proclaimed in the light of the newly-lit paschal candle. Of the seven prescribed, the first three are indispensable. These relate the foundational events of salvation history and provide the images through which Christ's paschal mystery is interpreted. Moreover, the two readings from Genesis and the passage from Exodus are hallowed by their use in the earliest Eastern and Roman traditions of the vigil. The Exodus 14 story of God's mighty act of freeing the Hebrew people from Egyptian slavery is the most important of the designated Old Testament passages. Already in the second century, Christian tradition had paired Jesus' passage through death to risen glory with Israel's passage through the waters of the Red Sea from slavery to freedom. Now proclaimed in the context of the Easter vigil, the prime occasion for the Church's celebration of initiation, the story of the Exodus becomes a *type* of Christian baptism—a *type* being an Old Testament event whose pattern and configuration foreshadow a New Testament reality. Just as crossing the Red Sea resulted in the creation of a people freed from slavery, passing through the waters of baptism creates a new humanity in Christ redeemed from the powers of sin and death. So central is this Exodus story that the Paschal Proclamation (the *Exsultet*), sung at the outset of the vigil, gleans dozens of images and phrases from this key episode in the history of salvation.

Next in importance are the two Genesis selections. The creation of Adam and Eve foreshadows the new creation inaugurated by the resurrection of Jesus, the second Adam. This creation motif correlates well with

---

[3]*Origins* 17/40 (March 17, 1988) 677–87.

Exodus 14, for just as in Genesis God created the world out of the watery chaos, in Exodus God led the Hebrew people through the waters of death (the Red Sea) to a new life in freedom as the chosen people. In Genesis 22, Abraham's willingness not to spare his son Isaac is a foreshadowing of God who did not spare his own son, but allowed him to be delivered unto death for the salvation of the world.

The prophetic texts rank third. Each speaks in its own way of God's promise of redemption and of a renewed covenant in the wake of the most traumatic period of the Jewish people's history: the destruction of Jerusalem and its temple, and the carrying off of the people into the Babylonian Exile. In the context of the vigil, these passages proclaim that God's promises are realized for all peoples and for all time in the death and resurrection of Jesus. If for pastoral reasons all four texts cannot be read, in Year A the fifth and seventh readings are recommended because of their use of water images evoking baptism. In Year B, the sixth reading is recommended. Here the prophet Baruch broaches themes similar to those featured in the second readings of the Sundays of Easter from the First Letter of John. The fourth reading would be particularly apropos for Year C. In this excerpt Isaiah speaks of the New Jerusalem, an image which will reappear on the Sixth Sunday of Easter in Year C.

More than any other biblical text, the New Testament passage from Romans 6:3-11 has left its imprint on the interpretation of baptism and on the development of baptismal ceremonial in the West. It plays an essential role in the vigil because it serves as the commentary *par excellence* on the rite of baptism celebrated immediately following the Liturgy of the Word. Paul's language of dying with Christ and being buried with him so as one day to share in a like resurrection describes baptism as the ritual through which candidates appropriate Christ's paschal mystery. This text, which most probably envisions baptism by immersion, echoes key themes in the Old Testament readings proclaimed at the vigil: candidates are plunged into the waters of chaos (the creation story), of death (the story of the flood), and of slavery (the story of Exodus), to emerge as a new creation in Christ, freed from the power of death and the slavery of sin.

The gospel passage recounts the women's discovery of the empty tomb. The episode reaches its climax in the angel's proclamation that Jesus has been raised from the dead. While all the other readings remain the same for all three Lectionary years, the gospel is the exception. It follows the general Lectionary pattern of Matthew for Year A, Mark for Year B, and Luke for Year C. At long last, after an evening of waiting, watching, and praying, the good news is proclaimed in words drawn from the gospel itself, the Church's most sacred text. God's victory in Christ over the powers of sin and death fulfills the long story of salvation, a history reaching back to creation and stretching to the end of time until the general resurrection from the dead. This is the good news that transforms Christians into a new humanity, the proclamation that calls them to gather as Church. Having once again heard the story of salvation proclaimed in the Liturgy of the Word, the assembled believers can then proceed to perform the sacred actions of baptism and Eucharist through which they enter into the paschal mystery of Christ.

One final note needs mention regarding this most holy night. As the apex of the Church's liturgical experience, the vigil provides the paradigm, the fundamental pattern, of all liturgy. This paradigmatic function applies to the Liturgy of the Word as well: the way the Easter vigil appropriates and interprets the scriptures establishes the basic approach for how the liturgy always and everywhere deals with the scriptures. At the vigil the gospel represents in essence what the gospel passage is at every celebration—a proclamation of the good news of God's victory over sin and death through Christ, "who was handed over to death for our trespasses and was raised for our justification" (Rom 4:25). The excerpt from Paul illustrates the role of the apostolic writings. They interpret the meaning of the paschal mystery and show how the earliest Christians appropriated it in their lives, giving warrant for today's Christian communities to do the same. The series of Old Testament passages, read in the light of Christ flaming in the paschal candle, not only recounts the story of which Jesus is the protagonist but also continues today what the risen Christ once did with the disciples of Emmaus: "Then beginning with Moses and all the prophets he interpreted to them the things about himself in all the scriptures" (Luke 24:27).

Mass of the Lord's Supper

The Lectionary selects the following passages for Thursday of the Easter triduum:

	Years A, B, C
First reading	Exodus 12:1-8; 11-14**
Second reading	1 Corinthians 11:23-26*
Gospel	John 13:1-15*

* readings retained from the *MR* 1570
** this passage was read on Good Friday in the *MR* 1570

The triduum celebration of the paschal mystery opens with the commemoration of the Lord's Last Supper on the night before he died. All three biblical passages selected for this sublime occasion together offer a rich feast of images endowing the celebration with the depth and significance it merits. Just as the Book of Exodus is indispensable at the vigil, so also here the passage from Exodus 12 provides the historical depth against which the Last Supper attains its full significance. The reading from Paul's First Letter to the Corinthians, like the excerpt from Romans at the vigil, plays a crucial role in interpreting Jesus' words and actions at the Last Supper. By drawing the gospel excerpt from John, the Lectionary links this celebration with the Johannine passion read on Good Friday, as well as with the Sundays of Lent and the Sundays of Easter, most of which draw their gospel passages from John. In order to highlight the principle of correspondence, the characteristic trait of the triduum Lectionary, the following examination of the readings for the Mass of the Lord's Supper and for the celebration of the Lord's passion will proceed in the order of gospel, apostolic writing, and Old Testament.

John 13:1-15. As the gospel passage for the first liturgical celebration of the triduum, the Lectionary proposes the footwashing episode drawn from John's account of the Last Supper. The passage contains two parts: Jesus washes the disciples' feet (13:2-11), and Jesus enjoins the disciples to do the same to one another (13:12-15).

In his opening comments John hints at the meaning of Jesus washing his disciples' feet (v.1). It is not a matter of coincidence that this particular *Passover* is Jesus' hour, the moment destined for Jesus to *pass* from this world to return to the Father. Passing from this world means dying, and Jesus accomplishes this dying by "loving his own to the end." To illustrate this, John then proceeds to recount Jesus' action of washing his disciples' feet. The incident serves as an enacted parable of Jesus loving his own to the end, for the words used to describe Jesus taking off his outer garment (v. 4) and then putting it on again (v. 12) are the same words spoken by the Good Shepherd who lays down his life for the sheep, only to take it up again (John 10:17).

At the time of Jesus, washing a guest's feet was a mark of hospitality usually performed by the household servants. In the absence of servants, the host fulfilled the task. By performing the gesture, Jesus, in lowering himself to the form of a slave, offers a two-pronged invitation to his disciples. First, as their servant, he invites them to join in similar self-giving by serving one another. This is explained in the second part of the episode where Jesus enjoins his disciples to wash each other's feet. As a result, footwashing becomes for Christians an enacted parable of the new commandment, "Love one another (i.e., be self-giving toward one another, symbolized by washing each other's feet) as I have loved you (i.e., to the end, as I have signified by washing your feet)" (15:12). Second, as their host, Jesus invites them to join him one day in his Father's house, where he is going to prepare a place for them (14:2). Self-giving, therefore, is the way Jesus and those who follow him journey from this world to the Father.

Finally, the dialogue between Jesus and Peter about washing, particularly Peter's retort "not only my feet but also my hands and my head," contains baptismal overtones, anticipating the vigil's celebration of initiation. Baptism is the pledge to imitate Jesus in his service to others, a service which is self-giving "to the end," to die with Christ so as one day to be raised with him (Romans 6, read at the vigil). Thus do Christians appropriate the paschal mystery of Jesus.

1 Corinthians 11:23-26. The gospel story of the footwashing sheds light on the second reading of the day, an excerpt from Paul's account of the Last Supper in 1 Corinthians 11. This short passage is the earliest recorded version of Jesus' words of blessing over the bread and the cup on the night before he died. Although there is no mention of crucifixion or death, the passage is replete with sacrificial language and imagery. All the animal sacrifices of Israel, no matter what immediate ritual purpose they might serve, had in common the separating of the blood from the victim's body. After the sacrificial animal's throat had been slit, the blood was gathered into a bowl and then poured out on the altar of sacrifice; the carcass or parts of the carcass were then burned, roasted, or boiled. By using the words "my body" in blessing the bread and "my blood" in blessing the cup, Jesus clearly intended to connote his sacrificial death. Thus Jesus' self-giving, his loving his own "to the end," symbolized by his stooping down to wash his disciples' feet, was to be accomplished through his sacrificial death on the cross.

By replacing the narrative of Jesus' blessing over the bread and the cup with the episode of Jesus washing his disciples' feet, John suggests that the meaning of Eucharist is lived in service to others. The Lectionary hints at the same correlation by pairing the gospel of the footwashing with Paul's version of the Last Supper. Indeed, Paul himself explicates the link between meal and self-giving in the verses immediately following today's selected passage where he reminds the Corinthian community that to celebrate the Lord's Supper worthily they must "discern the body." They must realize that not only the bread and wine are Jesus' body and blood but that also their brothers and sisters—rich or poor, slave or free, Jew or Gentile—are the body of Christ. If not treating the bread and wine with due respect is failing to discern the Lord's body, not recognizing in those gathered at the table the brother or sister for whom Christ died (1 Cor 8:11) also fails to discern the Lord's body.

Exodus 12:1-8, 11-14. The first reading from Exodus unfolds further the themes and images contained especially in the gospel reading. Exodus 12 recounts the well-known story of the Israelites' preparing and celebrating the original passover meal on the eve of their crossing the Red Sea. Each family was to select a lamb, immolate it, roast it, and eat it in haste in anticipation of the escape from Egypt. Before eating the lamb, the Israelites marked the doorposts and lintels of their houses with the blood of the lamb. The destroying angel, seeing the *blood* on the *wood*, would *pass over* their houses and strike only the firstborn of the Egyptians.

In the opening verse of the gospel reading, John makes it clear that the events to follow—the Last Supper, the passion, the crucifixion—take place at Passover. In addition, unlike the other three evangelists, John twice specifies that Jesus' crucifixion took place in the afternoon of Preparation Day when thousands of passover lambs were being immolated at the temple in Jerusalem. In so doing, John signifies that Jesus is the true *passover* sacrifice, the lamb of God who, through his *blood* shed on the *wood* of the cross, takes away the sins of the world.

Jewish tradition, which early Christian writers knew well, suggests yet other links between Exodus 12 and the interpretation of Jesus' paschal mystery. The Lectionary exploits these links in its selection and distribution of readings for the triduum, as the following instance illustrates. God's sparing of the firstborn of the Israelites by *passing over* their houses marked with blood inevitably evoked the story of God sparing Abraham from sacrificing his son Isaac on Mt. Moriah. Jewish tradition linked the two stories by identifying Mt. Moriah with Mt. Sion, the spur of land on which the temple in Jerusalem stood and where on Preparation Day the passover lambs were slaughtered. Christians saw in Jesus crucified not only the true passover lamb, the Lamb of God, but also the son whom God did not spare. Thus the Old Testament readings for the triduum weave a tapestry of foreshadowings that will come to pass in the paschal mystery of Christ.

Celebration of the Lord's Passion

Along with the Mass of the Lord's Supper, the Celebration of the Lord's Passion takes place on the first and same day of the triduum. The supper, after sundown on Thursday, ritually anticipates what will take place in the crucifixion; the passion, on Friday afternoon, fully authenticates what was said at the supper. In this way the Lectionary underlines the unity of the paschal mystery.

For the Friday commemoration of the Lord's passion, the Lectionary proposes the following readings:

Years A, B, C

First reading	Isaiah 52:13–53:12
Second reading	Hebrews 4:14-16; 5:7-9
Gospel	John 18:1–19:42*

* readings retained from the *MR* 1570

John 18:1–19:42. The reading of the passion according to John, a tradition firmly established in the *Missale Romanum* of 1570, probably dates back to the earliest centuries of the Church. A comparison between John's account and those of the synoptics justifies the liturgy's enduring preference for the former in celebrating the Lord's passion.

Contrary to the synoptics, John's passion account has no agony of Jesus in the garden, no kiss of Judas or flight of the disciples, no trial before the Sanhedrin, no flogging at the high priest's house or at Herod's, no mockery by the crowd at the crucifixion, no cry of dereliction from the cross, no darkness covering the land at Jesus' death, no episode of the good thief, and no story of the death of Judas. Instead, John's narrative adds several unique episodes: in Gethsemane, all Jesus' enemies fall down when he says the words "I am"; in his two trials Jesus is no longer silent, but engages in dialogues with Annas, the high priest, and with Pilate, the Roman procurator; there is discussion about what Pilate had written on the cross; a citation from Psalm 21 explains the casting of lots over Jesus' garment; Mary and the beloved disciple stand at the foot of the cross; and finally, a soldier pierces Jesus' side, from which flow blood and water.

All of these omissions and additions conspire to create John's particular theological portrait of Jesus. Here Jesus is not a passive victim acted upon by the powers of this world. At every turn he is the master of his fate. Nothing happens to him or to his disciples unless he gives permission or allows it. His submitting to suffering and death is so fully aligned with the Father's will that already glory and vindication shine through. The way of the cross takes on the trappings of a triumphal procession; a public execution becomes a forum proclaiming God's judgment and vindication; the cross, Jesus' throne of glory. Even the calm cadence and measured pacing of John's syntax betrays total confidence in God's victory. John's passion account is not so much about the cross as it is about the cross transformed into a sign of salvation. By being lifted up, Jesus realized "loving his own to the end," a destiny he had foreshadowed by washing the disciples' feet. In light of Exodus 12, as the liturgy suggests, and against the background of Preparation Day, as John intimates, the crucified Jesus is the passover sacrifice, the Lamb of God who takes away the sins of the world. In him the Jewish feast of Passover is transformed once and for all. Thus, John's inimitable way of knitting a narrative so rich in images and symbols clearly makes his passion account the most fitting one for proclaiming the paschal mystery on Friday of the triduum.

Hebrews 4:14-16; 5:7-9. Passers-by and onlookers at Golgotha would never have interpreted Jesus' crucifixion as a sacrifice; for them the event was merely the execution of just another criminal condemned to die a slave's opprobrious death. In light of the resurrection, however, Christian tradition did not hesitate to interpret Jesus' death as a sacrifice, but a sacrifice so rich in meaning that it stretched traditional images of sacrifice beyond their limits. Just as John's passion paradoxically merges suffering and glory into a sublime unity, the author of Hebrews presents Jesus as both sacrificial victim and sacrificer.

Such clauses as ". . . one who in every respect has been tested as we are . . .," "he offered up prayers and supplications, with loud cries and tears . . .," and "although he was a Son, he learned obedience through what he suffered . . .," underscore Jesus as sacrificial offering. The focus of today's selection from Hebrews, however, lies more on Jesus as priest, the mediator of the sacrifice. In Jewish liturgical tradition, only once a year, on the Day of Atonement, could the high priest enter the Holy of Holies in the temple at Jerusalem to offer expiation for Israel's sins. The author of Hebrews sees in Jesus' offering of himself in obedience unto death the perfect sacrifice that makes him the high priest who can now enter, not the Holy of Holies once a year, but the very presence of God for all time. As a result the risen Christ is *the* high priest who can intercede for us as no other high priest ever could. Only God's life-giving power could transform the public execution of a man into the perfect realization of Israel's holiest liturgy. Through these exalted images the Letter to the Hebrews discloses the significance of the paschal mystery.

Isaiah 52:13–53:12. If in the book of the prophet Isaiah Hebrew poetry attains its zenith, the Fourth Song of the Suffering Servant is doubtless the pinnacle of the book itself. Most probably Isaiah intended the servant in the poem to represent the people of Israel, particularly those who had suffered the Exile, and yet who continued to trust that God would one day vindicate their faithfulness. Throughout the centuries Jewish and Christian readers interpreted the servant as standing for the countless number of voiceless, innocent victims of war and oppression.

Without denying the universal reach of the poem, from the very beginning Christian tradition recognized in the Servant Song an uncannily evocative description of Jesus' passion, death, and resurrection. Nearly every verse of the passage applies directly to Jesus: "a man of suffering . . . wounded for our transgressions . . . a lamb led to the slaughter . . . he poured out himself to death." By pairing the poem with both John's passion narrative and the passage from Hebrews, the liturgy suggests that, just as surely as Jesus was vindicated in his suffering and death by being raised to new life, so also will God vindicate all victims of suffering and oppression. By selecting this poem as part of the triduum celebration, the Lectionary intimates that the paschal mystery embraces all of humankind.

All three biblical passages for the Celebration of the Lord's Passion present the paschal mystery in both its aspects of death and resurrection. All three readings, all the while unflinchingly presenting suffering and death, radiate with the glory of God's unfailing love and vindication.

Resurrection of the Lord—Easter Sunday

Easter Sunday basks in the splendor of the resurrection proclaimed at the vigil. This comes as no surprise, for both the vigil and Sunday celebrate the one paschal mystery and together constitute the third and last day of the triduum. Easter Sunday also serves as the hinge between the triduum and the Great Fifty Days of the Easter season. It looks back by pointing out that it is the *crucified* and *buried* Jesus who has been raised; it looks ahead by establishing the basic patterns of scripture readings characterizing the Sundays of Easter.

The readings for Easter Sunday are as follows:

	Years A, B, C
First reading	Acts 10:34, 37-43
Second reading	Colossians 3:1-4 or 1 Corinthians 5:6-8*
Gospel	John 20:1-9 (or 1-18 in Canada)

* reading retained from the *MR* 1570

John 20:1-9 or 1-18. The gospel passage—the Johannine version of the discovery of the empty tomb (vv. 1-9, the shorter passage)—directly links the Easter Sunday gospel with the gospel proclaimed at the vigil a few hours earlier. The longer version (vv. 1-18) happily includes the deeply moving story of Jesus' appearance to Mary Magdalene, who had mistaken him for the gardener.

The story opens with notations of time and place already familiar from the synoptics: it is early (but here more precisely it is "still dark") on the morning of the first day of the week. John individualizes the incident and thus renders it more intimate by reducing the number of women in the synoptic accounts to Mary Magdalene only. Her role here is to set in motion the sequence of events leading to the discovery of the empty tomb. This she does not only by being the first to visit the tomb but also by supplying the first, yet erroneous, interpretation of its meaning. Her supposition that someone has removed Jesus' body (repeated later in vv. 13 and 15) also demonstrates that she had no expectation of the resurrection.

Peter and the other disciple, upon hearing Mary's announcement, race to the tomb. John adds the curious detail that the other disciple arrived first. This latter peers in, sees "the linen wrappings lying there," but defers to Peter who then enters the tomb to find the same linen cloths just mentioned, along with "the cloth that had been on Jesus' head, not lying with the linen wrappings but rolled up in a place by itself." John's attention to detail is not fortuitous. First, the "linen wrappings lying there" invalidate Mary's supposition: grave robbers would neither have taken the time nor have made the effort to unravel a tightly wrapped corpse in order to spirit it away. Second, contrary to the raising of Lazarus who emerged from the tomb still bound, Jesus in his resurrection is freed from all bonds. Finally, the facial cloth "not lying with the linen wrappings but rolled up in a place by itself" shows the full power and majesty of the Johannine Jesus who on his own initiative can lay down his life and take it up again (10:18). Once again, as he does throughout his gospel, John subtly hints at the ineffable. Just as the cross is paradoxically both the instrument of Jesus' death and the throne of his exaltation, here the banal trappings of death become signs of resurrection: the tomb is empty, the linen cloth is folded. Death and resurrection—the paschal mystery.

The other disciple enters, *sees* what Simon Peter sees, and *believes*. John does not comment on Peter's faith, but it is clear that he gives the primacy of belief in the resurrection to the other disciple. For without having seen the risen Christ, he *believed* on the strength alone of the signs of the cloths in the empty tomb. Thus the other disciple becomes the first to live out the beatitude the risen Christ later speaks to Thomas: "Blessed are those who have not seen [me] and yet have come to believe" (John 20:29b, read on the Second Sunday of Easter, Years A,B,C). Signs correctly interpreted transform doubt into faith.

While the first episode describes disciples coming to faith, the second episode relates the appearance of the risen Jesus to an individual and of her coming to faith. Mary Magdalene's mistaken identification of Jesus as the gardener points out that as a result of his resurrection the Lord has been transformed and can no longer be recognized merely by sight. She recognizes Jesus when he speaks her name, that is, she hears (the word of) the Lord. This tender scene dramatizes Jesus' words in the parable of the Good Shepherd: ". . . the sheep hear his voice. He calls his own sheep by name and he leads them out" (John 10:3, read on the Fourth Sunday of Easter, Year A). Upon Jesus' calling her name, Mary Magdalene's grief is transformed into joy. Hearing the word (the scriptures) and seeing the signs (bread and wine), that is, celebrating the Sunday Eucharist, is still the way for assemblies today to come to believe that Christ is risen.

Colossians 3:1-4 or 1 Corinthians 5:6b-8. The reading from Colossians harkens back to the passage from Paul's Letter to the Romans proclaimed at the vigil. In Romans 6:4 Paul explained how "we have been buried with him by baptism into death, so that, just as Christ was raised from the dead by the glory of the Father, so we too might walk in newness of life." Colossians unfolds Paul's imagery even further by stating that believers have already been raised with Christ, albeit in a hidden way. The fullness of this risen life, begun in baptism, will be revealed at the Lord's coming in glory; then all will be made like him as he is. In evoking the theme of eschatological glory, this passage from Colossians points ahead to the selections from the Book of Revelation read as second reading for the Sundays of Easter Year C.

The short excerpt from 1 Corinthians contains the only explicit mention in all of Paul's letters of Christ as the paschal lamb. By selecting this pericope the Lectionary alludes to the celebrations of the Lord's Supper and of the Lord's passion, where passover motifs figured so highly. If Christ is the paschal lamb, Christians, continues Paul, are the unleavened bread of the new Passover. Thus Paul transforms passover traditions to make them speak of the new Passover that God has accomplished in raising Jesus from the dead, a passing over not merely from slavery to freedom, but from death to new life. The Eucharist is the new passover meal now shared at the Lord's table.

Acts 10:34a, 36-43. The Lectionary further underlines the newness Christ brings by replacing the Old Testament reading with a passage from the Acts of the Apostles, a pattern maintained throughout the Sundays of Easter. Reading from Acts of the Apostles during the Easter season recalls that the Church emerged in history as a consequence of the death and resurrection of Christ.

The clause "to us . . . who ate and drank with him after he rose from the dead" recommends today's selection for Easter Sunday Eucharist, when Christians too gather to eat and drink with the risen Lord. The verse appears as part of the homily Peter preached just prior to baptizing Cornelius and family, the first Gentiles to join the Way, as the young Church was then called. Peter's homily features the Easter kerygma in the form of a condensed retelling of the key events configuring the paschal mystery. Although not included in today's excerpt, the sequel in Acts 10:44-48 can be called the Pentecost for Gentiles, for while Peter was still speaking, "the Holy Spirit fell on all who heard the word" (v. 44b). Even Gentiles receive the Spirit, the one and same Spirit with which God anointed Jesus of Nazareth (v. 38), which fell upon the disciples gathered in the upper room (Acts 2), and which labors even now to shape believers into the image and likeness of the risen Christ.

Conclusion

The Easter triduum Lectionary offers a rich collection of biblical passages to help worshippers "comprehend . . . what is the breadth and length and height and depth" of the mystery of Christ (Eph 3:18). The Lectionary pairs these excerpts in patterns that foster mutual illumination among the readings, underlining how ancient Jewish traditions and images become transformed in light of the paschal mystery. In the Easter triduum the liturgy paces the assembly through these transformations because it seeks above all to increase faith so that those who celebrate these sacred mysteries might be transformed into the image and likeness of Christ, crucified and risen.

5   The Easter Season

The *General Norms for the Liturgical Year and the Calendar* offers but a short description of the Easter season:

> The fifty days from Easter Sunday to Pentecost are celebrated in joyful exultation as one feast day, or better as one "great Sunday" (no. 22).

> The Sundays of this season rank as the paschal Sundays and, after Easter Sunday itself, are called the Second, Third, Fourth, Fifth, Sixth, and Seventh Sundays of Easter. The period of the fifty sacred days ends on Pentecost Sunday (no. 23).

The simple, unimposing tone of these words belies their immense importance. They articulate major shifts in the Church's conception of Eastertide by giving renewed prominence to ancient traditions reaching back to the third and fourth centuries. What Sunday is to the Christian week—the day of the resurrection, the day of the Lord, the inauguration of the New Creation—the Easter season is to the liturgical year. The Easter season, then, is Sunday writ large and amplified to embrace a period of fifty days stretching from Easter Sunday to Pentecost. In the early centuries of Christianity, before there were separate feasts of Ascension and Pentecost, the Fifty Days from Easter to Pentecost sought, "like the Lord's Day, [to] proclaim the lordship of Jesus as attested by his resurrection, ascension, and bestowal of the Spirit."[1]

The importance of the Fifty Days is further accentuated by the reform of the catechumenate. The revised *Rite of Christian Initiation of Adults* calls the Sundays of the Easter season the "period of postbaptismal catechesis or mystagogy," a time for the community and the newly-baptized together "to grow in deepening their grasp of the paschal mystery and in making it part of their lives through meditation on the Gospel, sharing in the Eucharist, and doing the works of charity" (*RCIA*, no. 234).

[1]Patrick Regan, "The Fifty Days and the Fiftieth Day," *Worship* 55 (1981) 215.

The Lectionary has a major role to play here, for the scriptural readings for the Sunday Masses of the Easter season provide one of the basic sources of catechesis, as the instructions for the rite specify:

> Besides being occasions for the newly baptized to gather with the community and share in the mysteries, these celebrations include particularly suitable readings from the Lectionary, especially the readings for Year A. Even when Christian initiation has been celebrated outside the usual times, the texts for these Sunday Masses of the Easter season may be used (no. 237).

The Lent-Easter cycle, therefore, with the Forty Days functioning as a pre-baptismal retreat and the Fifty Days as a period of post-baptismal catechesis, embraces all the facets of the journey of conversion leading to initiation, for it is through baptism that believers are immersed in and sealed with the paschal mystery of Christ.

In light of this return to the tradition of Eastertide as one "great Sunday," paragraph 23 of the *GNLYC* explains that the Sundays between Easter and Pentecost are no longer called Sundays *after* Easter, as though Easter Sunday alone celebrated the resurrection, but Sundays *of* Easter. Each Sunday of the season, then, is an integral part of the celebration of the resurrection.

Principles of Reading Selection and Distribution

The season of Easter is a festal season. As for all festal seasons, the main principle of reading selection is harmony, through which the liturgy selects biblical books and passages that are deemed most appropriate. In the case of Eastertide, ancient liturgical tradition manifested a predilection for the gospel according to John, the Acts of the Apostles, the First Letter of Peter, the First Letter of John, and the Book of Revelation. From these books the liturgy selects passages consonant with the themes of Easter. One special feature of the Sundays of Easter is the replacing of the Old Testament reading with passages from the New Testament's Acts of the Apostles. In this way the Lectionary underlines the emergence of the Church as witness to the newness of God's initiative in inaugurating the Age to Come through the death and resurrection of Jesus.

Once key passages are chosen, the Lectionary orders them according to three modalities: thematic groupings, semicontinuous reading, and correspondence. Thematic groupings appear in the selection and distribution patterns of the first reading and of the gospel; semicontinuous reading, broadly conceived, structures the patterns of the first and second readings. Due to the combination of thematic groupings and semicontinuous reading, the first readings from Acts, the second readings from the apostolic writings (1 Peter in Year A, 1 John in Year B, and Revelation in Year C), and the gospels each follow their own track across the season from the Second through to the Seventh Sundays of Easter. As a result, correspondence is the least represented of the three modalities of *lectio selecta* in this festal seasons. However, in addition to the feasts of Ascension and Pentecost where it is very prominent, correspondence nevertheless can be found on a number of Sundays between two, and sometimes among all three, readings.

Gospel Readings for the Easter Season[2]

Sunday	**Year A**	**Year B**	**Year C**
Second	John 20:19-31*	John 20:19-31	John 20:19-31
Third	Luke 24:13-35	Luke 24:35-48	John 21:1-19
Fourth	John 10:1-10	John 10:11-18*	John 10:27-30
Fifth	John 14:1-12	John 15:1-8	John 13:1, 31-33a,34-35
Sixth	John 14:15-21	John 15:9-17	John 14:23-29
Ascension	Matthew 28:16-20	Mark 16:15-20*	Luke 24:46-53
Seventh	John 17:1-11	John 17:11-19	John 17:20-26
Pentecost Vigil**	John 7:37-39	John 7:37-39	John 7:37-39
Pentecost	John 20:19-23	John 15:26-27; 16:12-15	John 14:15-16, 23b-26

* readings retained from the *MR* 1570
** The Lectionary provides reading selections for the Pentecost vigil (for an extended vigil, see note at the end of this chapter). However, on the eve of Pentecost Sunday, most parishes celebrate the Sunday Mass of Pentecost.

The gospel selections for the seven-week span of the Sundays of Easter are organized in thematic groupings that provide a strong note of

[2]The lists of readings in this and subsequent tables follow the Canadian *Lectionary: Sundays and Solemnities* (Ottawa: CCCB, 1992), which at times slightly adapts the listings found in *Ordo Lectionum Missae. Editio Typica Altera* (Città del Vaticano: Libreria Editrice Vaticana, 1981).

continuity from year to year in the three-year cycle of readings. In all three years, the gospels for the Second and Third Sundays of Easter recount stories of the risen Christ's appearances. The excerpt for the Second Sunday of Easter, repeated in all three Lectionary years, tells the story of "Doubting Thomas." It was selected to be read on this Sunday because, according to the indications provided in the text itself, the episode occurred "a week later" (John 20:26), that is, on the Sunday after the Lord's resurrection. The Third Sunday of Easter relates three different appearances of the risen Lord: to the disciples of Emmaus in Year A (Luke 24); to the eleven in Year B (Luke 24); to the disciples on the shore of the Sea of Galilee in Year C (John 21). These three passages have as unifying theme a meal shared between the disciples and the risen Christ. As a group these four appearance narratives proclaim the Easter good news that the Lord is risen.

The Fourth Sunday of Easter is dedicated to the theme of the Good Shepherd, a gospel image that became one of the most popular ways of depicting the risen Jesus in early Christian art and literature. On this Sunday the Lectionary presents the greater part of the tenth chapter of John's gospel, divided into three sequential sections, with one section read in each of the three Lectionary years. Although according to the story line of John's gospel Jesus preaches the Good Shepherd parable before his death and resurrection, the episode is nevertheless particularly apropos at Easter time. In this discourse Jesus himself interprets the meaning of his upcoming death and resurrection when he says: "The good shepherd lays down his life for his sheep . . . . I lay down my life in order to take it up again" (10:11, 17). The paschal motifs here are unmistakable.

The Fifth, Sixth, and Seventh Sundays of Easter offer excerpts from John's version of Jesus' farewell discourse at the Last Supper. For the Fifth Sunday are selected some of the most treasured words of Jesus, words whose full significance is revealed only in light of the resurrection: "I am the way, and the truth, and the life" (Year A); "I am the vine, you are the branches" (Year B); "I give you a new commandment, that you love one another" (Year C). The Sixth Sunday of Easter, Years A and C, presents Jesus' promise to send the Paraclete; in the selection for Year B, Jesus no longer calls his disciples servants but friends. The Lectionary assigns the prayer of Jesus for his disciples from John 17 to the Seventh Sunday of Easter, with the entire text divided into three segments distributed sequentially over the three Lectionary years.

Between the Sixth and Seventh Sundays of Easter, the Church celebrates the feast of the Ascension. On this feast the first reading from Acts of the Apostles, rather than the gospel excerpt, is constitutive of the feast. As a result, the same Lucan account of Jesus' ascension into heaven from Acts 2 is repeated in all three Lectionary years. The gospel excerpts, however, vary in each year of the three-year cycle according to the usual pattern: a passage from Matthew in Year A, a selection from Mark in Year B, and the shorter account of the ascension from the very end of Luke's gospel in Year C. These gospel passages amplify and elaborate various dimensions of Jesus' enthronement at the right hand of God, figurative language signifying that through his resurrection Jesus is exalted as Lord and thus shares fully in God's power. Through his resurrection, ascension, and exaltation, Jesus has been established henceforth as the only mediator between God and humankind.

For Pentecost Sunday, the 1969 edition of the Lectionary had assigned the same gospel passage (John 20:19-23) to all three years of the cycle. The revised 1981 edition has relegated this excerpt to Year A only, and provided Years B and C with their own selections: John 15:26-27, 16:12-15 and John 14:15-16, 23b-26, both of which contain Jesus' promise to send the Paraclete. These last two excerpts repeat verses that already appear on the Sixth Sunday of Easter Years B and A respectively. As much as the gospel readings for Years B and C are appropriate for the feast, the selection from John 20:19-23 in Year A best captures the original meaning of Pentecost as essentially an Easter celebration. According to this account Jesus breathed the Holy Spirit on his disciples on Easter Sunday evening, the very evening of the day he rose from the dead. Just as in Gen 2:7 God *breathes* into Adam's nostrils the breath of life and Adam becomes a *spirited* (= living) being, in the same way Jesus *breathes* his *Spirit* upon his disciples. The risen Lord is, like God in the Old Testament, the source of life, making of the disciples a new humanity, a new creation. This coordination of Pentecost with Easter is a return to early liturgical tradition which saw Pentecost not as a separate feast, but rather as the extension of Easter unto perfection, or, in biblical terms, as the "perfection of perfections" ("a week of weeks," i.e., 7 x 7 days + 1). With Pentecost, then, the Easter season comes full circle, forming one Great Sunday celebrated in the liturgical form of the Great Fifty Days.

The thematic groupings of gospel selections during Eastertide highlight two key aspects of the liturgy's celebration of the mystery of Jesus' resurrection. The first is the paradoxical interweaving of time and time-lessness; the second is the prominence given to eucharistic themes.

Time and timelessness. Regarding the interplay between time and timelessness, the *time* aspect is couched in the frame of fifty days that set the parameters of the Easter season. Among the New Testament authors, only Luke narrates the descent of the Spirit on the apostles as occurring on the Jewish feast of Pentecost, fifty days after Passover. It is from Acts, then, that the fourth-century Church found the inspiration for extending its liturgical celebration of Easter into a fifty-day period. From Acts also came the rationale for eventually instituting the Ascension and Pentecost as liturgical feasts in their own right, the first celebrated forty days after Easter, the second celebrated fifty days after Easter. This time frame has perdured throughout the centuries to the present. Because of this fifty-day time frame, in celebrating the Easter season the Christian community experiences time as progressing in a linear fashion, week by week, from Easter to Pentecost.

However, if on the one hand the shape of the Easter season creates a sense of time progressing, on the other hand the Lectionary counters the sense of linear time by underscoring the *timelessness* of the resurrection. Several observations gleaned from the content of the gospel passages bear this out:

- As mentioned above, the gospel passage for Pentecost Sunday in Year A, read fifty days *after* Easter, narrates Jesus giving the Spirit to his disciples on the very evening of Easter Sunday, the day of his resurrection. In addition, the same episode from John forms the first part of the gospel passage on the Second Sunday of Easter in all three years, a week *after* the resurrection.

- The two Lucan episodes of the appearances of the risen Christ (to the disciples of Emmaus and to the Eleven), are read on the Third Sunday of Easter, two weeks *after* Easter. According to Luke's indications, however, these appearances took place on the evening of Easter Sunday.

- According to John's gospel, Jesus' farewell discourse at the Last Supper, from which the Lectionary draws excerpts for the Fifth, Sixth, and Seventh Sundays in all three Lectionary years, took place *before* Jesus' death and resurrection. Yet the liturgy reads these passages *after* Easter. This is also the case for the gospel passages read on the Fourth Sunday of Easter from John 10 on the Good Shepherd. Although according to the story line of John's gospel all of these episodes occurred *before* the death and resurrection of Jesus, the liturgy assigns them to be read *after* Easter.

These observations demonstrate that, despite the fifty-day frame shaping the Easter season, even with the feasts of Ascension and Pentecost standing out as special celebrations, the liturgy is not simply commemorating the events surrounding the resurrection in their strict historical sequence. James Notebaart explains this liturgical mix of time and timelessness when he writes: "Easter's Fifty Days is a unit of time to be observed in its entirety rather than segments of a narrative to be looked at in some historical sequence. What we should be looking for is an insight into the meaning of the mystery, not a narrative of events." As the Church walks through Eastertide, then, "it is a mystery [it is] marking, not primarily events."[3] The mystery it is marking, of course, is always and everywhere the paschal mystery.

Eucharistic themes. The gospel readings for the season of Easter also give special prominence to the Eucharist. Most of the passages describe the disciples united with Jesus in the context of a meal. This is the case for all three selections for the Third Sunday of Easter—in each instance the risen Christ shares a meal with his disciples. In the gospel excerpts for the Fifth, Sixth, and Seventh Sundays of Easter, all drawn from the farewell discourse at the Last Supper, Jesus promises the disciples that he will continue to abide with them through their love for one another and through the gift of the Spirit. These passages suggest that the prime moment for the Christian assembly to commune with the risen Lord is at the Sunday Eucharist. The Sunday Eucharist is the moment *par excellence* when the assembly comes to the fullest consciousness of its identity as the body of Christ, the place where it realizes most clearly that the Age to Come is already emerging even in the midst of this world.

[3]James Notebaart, "The Paschal Season, The Days of Sunday," *Liturgy* 3/1 (Winter 1982) 11.

The First Reading from the Acts of the Apostles[4]

Sunday	Year A	Year B	Year C
Second	Acts 2:42-47	Acts 4:32-35	Acts 5:12-16
Third	Acts 2:14, 22b-28	Acts 3:13b-15, 17-19	Acts 5:27b-32, 40b-41
Fourth	Acts 2:14, 36-41	Acts 4:8-12	Acts 13:14, 43-52
Fifth	Acts 6:1-7	Acts 9:26-31	Acts 14:21b-27
Sixth	Acts 8:5-8, 14-17	Acts 10:25-26, 34-35, 44-48	Acts 15:1-2, 22-29
Ascension	Acts 1:1-11*	Acts 1:1-11	Acts 1:1-11
Seventh	Acts 1:12-14	Acts 1:15-17, 20ac, 20c-26	Acts 7:55-60
Pentecost Vigil**	Genesis 11:1-9 or Exodus 19:3-8a, 16-20b or Ezekiel 37:1-14 or Joel 3:1-5		
Pentecost	Acts 2:1-11*	Acts 2:1-11	Acts 2:1-11

     * readings retained from the *MR* 1570
     ** The Pentecost vigil is modeled after the Easter vigil, hence the introduction of Old Testament readings. For an extended Pentecost vigil, see note at the end of this chapter.

The Easter season is unique in being the only time when the Sunday and Feast Day Lectionary forgoes selections from the Old Testament. Although some members of the committee on Lectionary reform maintained that the joy of Easter could be found expressed in Old Testament passages, the return to the ancient Christian liturgical tradition of reading from the Acts of the Apostles at Easter prevailed. It is altogether fitting to evoke the birth and growth of the Church during this season, for the Church appears on the stage of history as a result of the resurrection of Jesus: ". . . we must remember that these narratives relate events in the life of the Church as it first came to terms with the reality of the resurrection of Jesus and with the reality of the content of the apostolic faith embodied in the kerygmatic preaching."[5]

---

[4]Much of this section is a revised version of my article "The Acts of the Apostles in the Easter Lectionary," *Celebrate!* 28/2 (March-April 1989) 8–10, which was largely based on Elmar Nübold, *Entstehung und Bewertung der neuen Perikopenordnung des römischen Ritus für die Messfeier an Sonn- und Festtagen* (Paderborn: Verlag Bonifatius-Druckerei, 1986) 337–41.

[5]"The Lectionary for Easter," *Liturgy* 3/1 (Winter 1982) 42.

As do the gospel passages for Eastertide, the selections from Acts play havoc with linear time. The seven-week period from Easter to Pentecost, based on the chronology found in Luke's Acts of the Apostles, lends to the liturgical community a sense of time progressing. However, the above table illustrates that linear time is not the paramount concern either of the liturgy or of the Lectionary. Even though the liturgical celebration of the granting of the Spirit on Pentecost is still weeks away, all the excerpts from the Second to the Sixth Sundays of Easter narrate events that, according to the plot of Acts, in fact took place *after* the Spirit had been bestowed. Only at the end of the Easter season, on the feast of the Ascension and on the Seventh Sunday of Easter, are the excerpts drawn from Acts 1, before Luke's account of the giving of the Spirit (with the one exception of Acts 7:55-60 in Year C).

This peculiar ordering of time provides clues for discerning the organizing pattern of the readings from Acts. First, since the Easter season is a festal season, the basic principle for choosing readings is harmony—passages are selected to express the theme or themes consonant with the season. In addition, at least from the Second through to the Sixth Sundays of Easter, the readings from Acts are arranged in a loose semicontinuous fashion to capture Luke's stage by stage sequence of the evolution of the Church. Although the passages are selected only from the first half of the story (chapters 1 to 15—Acts is 28 chapters long), the progression in the story from Sunday to Sunday becomes apparent in a listing of the chapter numbers from which excerpts have been drawn: Year A from chapters 2, 2, 2, 6, and 8; Year B from 4, 3, 4, 9, and 10; and Year C from 5, 5, 13, 14, and 15.

Beyond this nod to the modality of semicontinuous reading, a yet stronger pattern is the thematic unity of the three selections for each Sunday of Easter across the three Lectionary years. The three passages assigned to the Second Sunday of Easter, for example, describe the life of the earliest community: "[the disciples] devoted themselves to the apostles' teaching and fellowship . . . [they] had all things in common . . . . Day by day . . . they spent much time together in the Temple . . ." (Acts 2:42-47, Year A); they were "of one heart and soul . . . everything they owned was held in common . . . there was not a needy person among them . . .," (Acts 4:32-35, Year B); they "were all together in Solomon's Portico . . . the people held them in high esteem . . .," and "many signs and wonders were done among the people through the apostles" (Acts 5:12-16, Year C).

Speeches or sermons delivered by apostles, missionaries, and Church leaders constitute nearly one third of Acts. The Lectionary draws from this material for the Third and Fourth Sundays of Easter. The passages for the Third Sunday of Easter highlight the paschal mystery as proclaimed by Peter, the head of the apostles. Year A cites a passage from his Pentecost speech: "This man . . . handed over to you . . . you crucified and killed by the hands of those outside the law. But God raised him up" (Acts 2:23-24). Year B echoes the same proclamation from his address to the crowds at Solomon's Portico (Acts 3:11-26), and Year C invokes similar words spoken in defense of the apostles before the high priest (Acts 5:27-42).

The selection for the Fourth Sunday of Easter Year A quotes another excerpt from Peter's Pentecost sermon (Acts 2:14, 36-41), while in the excerpt for Year B the first of the apostles witnesses before the assembled leaders of the Jewish people (Acts 4:8-12). The selection for Year C turns to the ministry of Paul and Barnabas in a passage that joins the itinerant evangelizers on their first missionary journey (Acts 13:14, 43-52). After having been rejected in the synagogues, they turn to teaching and preaching among the Gentiles, another step toward the fulfillment of the risen Christ's prophecy that the apostles will be his witnesses "to the ends of the earth" (Acts 1:8).

The theme of call to service unites the selections for the Fifth Sunday of Easter. The appointment of the "seven men of good standing" to serve the community's needs forms the narrative for Year A (Acts 6:1-7). The passage for Year B focuses on service to the Word by relating the first preaching of the newly-converted Paul among the Greek-speaking Jews in Jerusalem (Acts 9:26-31). In Year C Paul and Barnabas name elders to serve as leaders in the several communities established during their first missionary journey (Acts 14:21b-27).

The Sixth Sunday of Easter targets the missionary expansion of the Church. In the selection for Year A, Philip proclaims the gospel in Samaria (Acts 8:5-8, 14-17). In Year B Peter baptizes Cornelius and his household (Acts 10:25-26, 34-35, 44-48), the first Gentiles to join the Church in a key event that sets the stage for the epochal "Jerusalem Council" recounted in Year C (Acts 15:1-2, 22-29).

For Ascension, the Seventh Sunday of Easter, and Pentecost, the Lectionary abandons its sequential and thematic reading of Acts to select episodes demanded by the feasts. The first reading on the Ascension narrates the story of Jesus' being taken up into heaven, a passage that, since it is constitutive of the feast, appears in all three Lectionary years. The selections for the Seventh Sunday of Easter describe the Jerusalem disciples' final preparations for the coming of the Spirit: they pray continually (Acts 1:12-14, Year A) and choose Matthias to replace Judas Iscariot (Acts 1:15-17, 20-26, Year B). The Year C selection adds another facet to the preparation-for-the-Spirit theme by citing the vision of Stephen, the first martyr, moments before his death: "I see the heavens opened and the Son of Man standing at the right hand of God" (7:55-60). The passage shows that indeed Jesus had ascended into heaven and is now poised to send his Spirit.

The Lectionary's final selection from Acts graces the feast of Pentecost, the closing celebration of the Easter season. As for the Ascension, the passage from Acts rather than the gospel is constitutive of the feast itself. The Spirit descending upon the twelve apostles in the perceptible forms of sound and fire recalls God's giving of the Law to Moses on Sinai, the main theme of the Jewish feast of Pentecost. Through these allusions to the scriptures Luke suggests that the Church, symbolized by the apostles, becomes the New Israel, a people guided by the Spirit rather than by the Law.

The Lectionary adds a special dimension to the Church's celebration of the resurrection through its selections of passages from the Acts of the Apostles. By evoking the Church's foundation and expansion at the Sunday Eucharists of Eastertide, the liturgy invites Christian communities to see themselves in the long lineage of faithful witnesses reaching back to the apostles. It also provides assemblies with the inspiration for proclaiming the good news in today's world and with the model for appropriating the paschal mystery of Christ in their lives.

Readings from the Apostolic Writings for the Easter Season

Sunday	Year A	Year B	Year C
Second	1 Peter 1:3-9	1 John 5:1-6*	Revelation 1:9-11a, 12-13, 17-19
Third	1 Peter 1:17-21	1 John 2:1-5	Revelation 5:11-14
Fourth	1 Peter 2:20-25*	1 John 3:1-2	Revelation 7:9, 14-17
Fifth	1 Peter 2:4-9	1 John 3:18-24	Revelation 21:1-5
Sixth	1 Peter 3:15-18	1 John 4:7-10	Revelation 21:10-14, 22-23

Sunday	Year A	Year B	Year C *(Con'd)*
Ascension	Ephesians 1:17-23	Ephesians 1:17-23 or Ephesians 4:1-13	Ephesians 1:17-23 or Hebrews 9:24-28;10:19-23
Seventh	1 Peter 4:13-16	1 John 4:11-16	Revelation 22:12-14, 16-17, 20
Pentecost Vigil**	Romans 8:22-27	Romans 8:22-27	Romans 8:22-27
Pentecost	1 Corinthians 12:3b-7, 12-13	1 Corinthians 12:3-7 or Galatians	1 Corinthians 12:3-7 or Romans 8:8-17

* readings retained from *MR* 1570
** See note at end of this chapter.

Consonant with ancient tradition, the Lectionary proposes readings from the First Letter of Peter, the First Letter of John, and the Book of Revelation during Eastertide. It has assigned selections from 1 Peter to Year A, from 1 John to Year B, from Revelation to Year C, and has distributed them according to a loose form of semicontinuous reading. Thus the second readings in all three Lectionary years follow each their own distinct track. Nevertheless, on a number of Sundays, and of course on the feasts of Ascension and Pentecost, the second readings correspond with either or with both of the other two readings.

The selections from the First Letter of Peter, probably an early post-baptismal homily, all display Easter themes and motifs. The passage on the Second Sunday speaks of baptism as a new birth; the texts on the Third, Fifth, and Sixth Sundays proclaim various aspects of the paschal mystery; the excerpt for the Fourth Sunday points out that Jesus is the shepherd and guardian of our souls; the selection for the Seventh Sunday tells how believers share in Jesus' sufferings and glory. In addition to these kerygmatic concerns, all of these passages carry a strong note of exhortation, explaining how believers are to behave toward each other and vis-à-vis the world, now that they have put on Christ.

Although the Year B passages from 1 John do not contain any explicit proclamation of the resurrection, they nevertheless surface a number of Easter motifs echoing John's version of the farewell discourse of Jesus, from which no fewer than twelve gospel passages have been drawn for the Sundays of Easter. The command to love one another, the exhortation to remain in God, the constant reminder that God dwells in believers—such are the manifestations of the paschal mystery of Jesus' death and resurrection in the lives of the faithful.

Selecting passages from the Book of Revelation in Year C follows an ancient precedent set by Milanese and Old Spanish traditions, in which this last book of the Bible replaced the Old Testament during the Easter season. The visions cited on the Second, Third, and Fourth Sundays depict Christ's Easter victory over the powers of sin and death: he is "the first and the last, the living one . . . [who has] the keys of Death and of Hades"; he is "the Lamb that was slaughtered to receive power and wealth and wisdom and might and honor and glory and blessing"; he is the Lamb who "will be their shepherd and will guide them to springs of the water of life." The visions read on the Fifth, Sixth, and Seventh Sundays conjure up the ultimate goal of this earthly pilgrimage: "the holy city, the new Jerusalem, coming down out of heaven from God," a city with no temple, for "its temple is the Lord God the Almighty and the Lamb," a city to which the "Spirit and the bride say, 'Come.'" First written to and for a persecuted Church, these visions encourage today's assemblies to persevere in the often difficult witnessing to and appropriation of the paschal mystery of Christ.

Given the separate tracks followed by each of the three readings, correspondence is the last and least important modality on the Sundays of Easter. Nevertheless, in a number of instances some form of relationship between two, sometimes among all three, readings can be detected. For example, on the Second Sunday Year A the reading from 1 Peter, "although you have not seen him, you love him," is well paired with the gospel episode of Doubting Thomas from John 20: "Blessed are those who have not seen and yet have come to believe. . . ." On the Fourth Sunday Year A the phrase from 1 Peter about Jesus being "the shepherd and guardian of your souls" matches well with the Good Shepherd gospel passage from John 10. Other examples of correspondence can be found throughout most of the Sundays of Year B and on the Second, Fourth, and Seventh Sundays in Year C.

The three selections proposed for the feast of the Ascension bring out different dimensions of Jesus' enthronement at God's right hand. The Year A reading from Ephesians 1 stresses Jesus' power over all earthly rule and dominion and describes him as the head of his body, the Church. In Year B, Ephesians 4 elaborates on the Christ-Church relationship, explaining that it is Christ the head of the Church who creates unity and makes the body grow. The passage from Hebrews for Year C develops the salvific aspects of Jesus' ascension. As *the* high priest, Christ enters, not the Holy of

Holies in the temple at Jerusalem, but the heavenly sanctuary not made by human hands and thus fulfills once for all the sacrifice that takes away sin.

As expected, the readings for Pentecost explore the many aspects of the Spirit's presence and work among believers. The Year A text from 1 Corinthians describes how, although believers have different gifts, all have been baptized in the one Spirit and are therefore one body. The Galatians passage for Year B lists the fruits of those who live according to the Spirit. In Year C the selection from Romans contrasts life in the flesh with life in the Spirit, stating that "all who are led by the Spirit of God are children of God" who in this Spirit can cry out "Abba! Father!"

Strangely enough, despite Paul's repeated insistence that he has seen the risen Lord, and despite his bequeathing to posterity some of the most deeply pondered reflections on Jesus' resurrection, the Lectionary cites no Pauline text on resurrection during the Sundays of Easter. The three passages from his letters selected for Pentecost Sunday have to do with the Spirit. The committee on Lectionary reform for the most part reserved the reading of Paul's letters for the Sundays in Ordinary Time. In this way they honored the reading of excerpts from other New Testament books that might otherwise have been neglected.

Conclusion

The Fifty Days, celebrated as one Great Sunday, underline the victorious, triumphant facet of the paschal mystery of Christ. They bask in an aura of the risen Lord's abiding presence with his Church, though it is still a hidden presence. They offer a foretaste of the heavenly kingdom where the faithful, clothed in white, will be gathered with the Lamb that was slain to give praise and glory to God. The Lectionary provides the stories and images and language with which the liturgy articulates the mystery so that the faithful can appropriate it in their lives, yearning to experience one day the fullness promised them by being transformed into the image and likeness of Jesus, crucified and risen.

Note on the Vigil of Pentecost

While the 1981 edition of the Lectionary, based on the *Editio Typica Altera* of the *Ordo Lectionum Missae*, makes provisions for a vigil of Pentecost, editions of the Sunday and Feast Day Lectionary published after 1988 include biblical selections for an extended vigil of Pentecost. This comes in the wake of directives contained in the Congregation for

Divine Worship's circular letter *Preparing and Celebrating the Paschal Feasts* (January 16, 1988):

> Encouragement should be given to the prolonged celebration of Mass in the form of a vigil whose character is not baptismal as in the Easter Vigil, but is one of urgent prayer, after the example of the apostles and disciples, who persevered together in prayer with Mary, the mother of Jesus, as they awaited the Holy Spirit (no. 107).[6]

The shorter vigil of Pentecost of the 1981 edition offers a choice of one of four Old Testament readings (Gen 11:1-9; Exod 19:3-8a, 16-20; Ezek 37:1-14; or Joel 2:28-31), a passage from the apostolic writings (Rom 8:22-27), and a gospel passage (John 7:37-39). The post-1988 extended vigil of Pentecost, patterned after the Liturgy of the Word for the Easter vigil, comprises nine readings in all, seven from the Old Testament, one from the apostolic writings, and a gospel excerpt:

First reading:	Genesis 2:4b-10, 18, 21-25 (the creation of Adam and Eve)
Second reading:	Genesis 11:1-9 (the Tower of Babel)
Third reading:	Exodus 19:3-8a, 16-20 (the preparation for the giving of the law on Mt. Sinai)
Fourth reading:	Proverbs 8:22-31 (personified Wisdom as God's master worker at creation)
Fifth reading:	Jeremiah 31:31-34 (the new covenant, written on the heart)
Sixth reading:	Ezekiel 37:1-14 (the dry bones that are made alive by the spirit)
Seventh reading:	Joel 2:18-32 (the spirit of God will be poured out on all flesh)
Epistle:	Romans 8:22-27 (the Spirit intercedes with sighs too deep for words)
Gospel:	John 7:37-39 (out of the believer's heart shall flow rivers of living water)

As the brief descriptions suggest, the biblical passages all focus on the Spirit of God, present and active from the beginning in creation, in key moments in the history of the people of Israel, and finally in Jesus who, in his exalted state at God's right hand, pours it out upon his Church that it might be spread to all peoples. Thus the Lectionary provides a marvellous sequence of texts for a prolonged meditation on the gift of the Spirit celebrated at Pentecost.

[6]*Origins* 17/40 (March 17, 1988) 677–87.

6   The Season of Lent

Lent, like every liturgical season, celebrates the paschal mystery. The *General Norms for the Liturgical Year and the Calendar* describes the season of Lent as "a preparation for the celebration of Easter. For the Lenten liturgy disposes both catechumens and the faithful to celebrate the paschal mystery: catechumens, through the several stages of Christian initiation; the faithful, through reminders of their own baptism and through penitential practices" (no. 27).

The Sundays of Lent, although incorporated into a penitential season, nevertheless retain the fundamental festal character of *Sunday*—the Day of the Lord, the day commemorating the resurrection, the first day of the new creation. Hence, on the Sundays of Lent, but not on the weekdays, penitential practices are set aside.

As a festal season preparing for Easter, Lent underscores the passion and death aspects of Jesus' paschal mystery, his *passing over* from death to new life. The believing community prepares for Easter through penance; catechumens appropriate the paschal mystery through baptism. Penance and baptism have constituted the season's profile since the fourth century. The penitential aspect emerged first. The earliest traces of what would become Lent began to appear in the second century. At that time, the rise of an annual commemoration of Jesus' resurrection on Easter Sunday fostered the development of a two-day fast on the preceding Friday and Saturday. The period of fasting and penance was first extended to include the week before Easter, then the three weeks prior to the feast, until in the fourth century it embraced a six-week period of forty days. Also in the fourth century, in order to deal with the unprecedented influx of new Christians, Lent acquired a baptismal orientation. During Lent the catechumens underwent their final preparation for initiation at the Easter vigil. While the penitential flavor of Lent has remained a perennial factor, its baptismal character had been almost totally lost from the early Middle Ages until Vatican II. The council's liturgical reform restored the baptismal orientation of Lent so that the season might regain the richness it had in antiquity. In fact, by naming it first, it gives it precedence. Through its selections of biblical readings, the revised Lectionary highlights both dimensions of this liturgical season.

Principles of Reading Selection and Distribution

Because Lent is a festal season, the basic principle for choosing biblical passages is harmony. To articulate the major themes of the season, the Lectionary casts a wide net through both the Old and New Testaments, as evidenced in the tables listed below. The only biblical book featured during Lent is the Gospel according to John, a tradition dating from at least the third century. Of the fifteen gospel excerpts needed to cover the first five Sundays of Lent across the three-year cycle, seven are drawn from John.

The two main reading distribution patterns are thematic groupings and correspondence. The Sundays of Lent display no semicontinuous sequences. Thematic groupings structure both the gospels and the Old Testament readings. Although they follow their own independent tracks across the five Sundays of Lent, the Old Testament passages and the gospel excerpts more often than not correspond to each other. The readings from the apostolic writings are not grouped thematically. Instead, correspondence links them to either or both of the other two readings.

Regarding the gospels, in each year of the cycle the passages for the First and Second Sundays form one subgroup, while the passages for the Third, Fourth, and Fifth Sundays form another. As a general overture to the season, the gospels for the First and Second Sundays of Lent recount the temptation and the transfiguration, with Matthew's version in Year A, Mark's in Year B, and Luke's in Year C. Each Lectionary year, however, offers a different thematic grouping for the Third, Fourth, and Fifth Sundays. In Year A, the three successive gospel excerpts, all from John, have a baptismal orientation. In Year B, the three passages, again all from John, focus on the paschal mystery of Christ. The gospel passages for Year C, two drawn from Luke and one from John, highlight the lenten themes of penance and conversion.

The Old Testament readings exhibit a pattern of their own. From the First to the Fifth Sundays, in each year of the cycle, the Lectionary offers a five-stage thumbnail sketch of salvation history. On the First Sunday appear passages dealing with the primeval era; on the Second Sunday, stories about God's promises to Abraham; on the Third, momentous incidents in the life of Moses; on the Fourth, key events between the Exodus and the Exile; on the Fifth, prophetic portrayals of end-time fulfillment.

Unlike the Easter season where excerpts from Paul are virtually absent, Lent draws most of its second readings from the Apostle's letters. The only exceptions are a passage from the First Letter of Peter on the First Sunday and a text from the Letter to the Hebrews on the Fifth Sunday, both in Year B.

Passion (Palm) Sunday, although it is in fact the sixth Sunday in Lent, stands apart from the other five both in structure and content. Regarding its place in the architecture of the season, it serves as the opening celebration of Holy Week. In terms of content, the distinguishing trait of this Sunday lies, as its name indicates, in the reading of the passion—Matthew's version in Year A, Mark's in Year B, and Luke's in Year C. Attached to the celebration is an introductory rite, dating from early medieval times, that features the proclamation of Jesus' triumphal entry into Jerusalem which is then ritualized in a procession with palms. Because it has patterns of its own, it will be discussed at the end of this chapter.

Gospel Readings for the Season of Lent

Sunday	Year A	Year B	Year C
First	Matthew 4:1-11*	Mark 1:12-15	Luke 4:1-13
Second	Matthew 17:1-9*	Mark 9:2-10	Luke 9:28-36
Third	John 4:5-42	John 2:13-25	Luke 13:1-9
Fourth	John 9:1-41	John 3:14-21	Luke 15:1-3, 11-32
Fifth	John 11:1-45	John 12:20-33	John 8:1-11
	* readings retained from the *MR* 1570		

The gospel selections set the tone not only for each Sunday but also for the lenten season as a whole. In each year of the three-year cycle, the gospel for the First Sunday of Lent recounts the temptation of Jesus, that of the Second Sunday, the transfiguration. Together these two Sundays orchestrate a prelude to the entire Lent-Easter cycle by highlighting the two fundamental aspects of Jesus' paschal mystery, his death and resurrection. The temptation story, symbolizing the struggle against the forces of sin and evil, evokes Jesus' passion and death. The episode nevertheless already foreshadows a victorious outcome, for Jesus succeeds in thwarting Satan's parries. The transfiguration, with its aura of transforming light, intimates

Jesus' glorified state after his resurrection. The episode is not about victory alone, however, for Jesus explains that he must first go to Jerusalem where he will suffer and die. The path to life passes through suffering and death. Thus both Sundays present the paschal mystery *in nuce*, the First accentuating the struggle, the Second pointing to its outcome.

For the Third, Fourth, and Fifth Sundays the Lectionary presents a different lenten theme in each of the three Lectionary years. In Year A three lengthy passages from John's gospel are assigned: the Samaritan woman at the well on the Third Sunday (John 4), the healing of the man born blind on the Fourth Sunday (John 9), and the raising of Lazarus on the Fifth Sunday (John 11). The choice and placement of this exceptional trilogy of texts is a striking example of the council's intent to restore the baptismal orientation of Lent. The precedent for the renewed prominence of these gospel stories harkens back to the fourth century when the Church first forged a link between Lent and the catechumenate.[1]

There is enough evidence to suggest that already in the third century the earliest traces of what would become Lent featured the reading of John's gospel, perhaps in a continuous form, certainly with special emphasis on chapters 4, 9, 11. As part of the penitential preparation for Easter, these three passages highlighted the Johannine themes of the political tensions at Passover time, of the plot to kill Jesus, and of the conflict between Jesus and the "world." In the early centuries of this era, the fledgling Church saw its own precarious situation reflected in Jesus' struggles. An outlawed movement that proclaimed the scandalous belief in a crucified man as Messiah and Savior of the world, it too met with opposition often erupting into persecution. In less tumultuous times, penitential practices helped believers participate in the struggle against the powers of sin and death that continue to enslave this world.

The same three chapters from John reveal yet other facets of Christian life, however. In relating stories of people coming to faith in Jesus, these narratives naturally evoked the journey of candidates toward baptism—conversion meant moving from sin (thirst) to grace (living water), from darkness (blindness) to light (sight), from death to resurrection. Although Lent-Easter had not yet become the special and exclusive liturgical season for celebrating baptism, the influence of these three passages from John's gospel already oriented the liturgy in that direction.

---

[1] The following paragraphs on the link between John 4, 9, and 11 and the scrutinies are a revised version of my article "The Scrutinies and the Gospel of John," *Celebrate!* 29/2 (March–April 1990) 9–12.

Prior to its incorporation into Lent in the fourth century, baptism was celebrated at any time throughout the year, usually on Sundays, although a preference for Eastertide slowly began to emerge. There was no organized or standardized catechumenate. The relatively few candidates who sought baptism were each assigned a sponsor and were prepared individually for a period of usually three or more years.

During the final weeks before baptism, candidates underwent an intense preparation that featured special prayers called "scrutinies." These took the form of exorcism-prayers through which the assembly asked God to remove all the enticements and influences of evil in the candidates and to purify them so that they might totally turn away from their former lives and thus freely enter the community of faith as people reborn. These prayers, then, despite the name "scrutinies," did not seek to evaluate a candidate's worthiness for baptism. That decision had been made earlier in the process. They functioned rather to encourage the candidates to open themselves fully to the transforming power of God as they left behind their old selves and "put on Christ."

With these two different and separate preparations, the preparation for Easter and the preparation for baptism, the fourth-century Church would create a marvelous alliance. In A.D. 313, the year after he became emperor, Constantine legalized Christianity. Near the end of the century one of his successors declared it the official religion of the Roman Empire. These events resulted in major changes within the Church. On the one hand, the new freedom allowed it to develop its liturgical life in peace and security, such as the expansion of the penitential preparation for Easter into a forty-day Lent. On the other hand, the elimination of persecution and the official establishment of Christianity encouraged an unprecedented influx of candidates seeking baptism. Faced with this challenge, the Church elaborated and standardized the preparation for baptism into a full-fledged catechumenate. In order to stress the importance of baptism as well as to assure greater order and efficiency in the initiation process, it seemed only logical that the final preparation for baptism with its special scrutinies should take place during the preparation for Easter with its baptism-oriented readings from John. And so the two originally distinct preparations converged to form an intensive "retreat" for candidates about to be baptized at the Easter vigil.

The merger of Lent's gospel passages from John 4, 9, and 11 with the catechumenate's scrutinies had the following effect: the scrutinies more and more took on the language and imagery of the gospel passages, while the gospel passages served to interpret the process of initiation. This felicitous union of word (gospel texts) and ritual (scrutinies) was so strong that it would survive centuries of neglect.

This baptismal orientation of Lent remained in force until approximately the end of the sixth century. By that time adult baptisms had diminished to a trickle; instead, infant baptisms had become the norm. The catechumenate, no longer needed to prepare adults for baptism, progressively declined until in the seventh century both the John readings and their attendant scrutinies for the Third, Fourth, and Fifth Sundays of Lent were relegated to lenten weekdays. John 4 appeared on Friday of the third week of Lent, John 9 on Wednesday of the fourth week of Lent, and John 11 on Friday of the fourth week of Lent. As the centuries moved on, the lenten season retained only vestiges of its original baptismal character.

The liturgical renewal of Vatican II has restored the baptismal significance of the Lent-Easter cycle, in great part by reinstating the catechumenate through its current adaptation called the *Rite of Christian Initiation of Adults* (*RCIA*). In turn, the recovery of the catechumenate has led the Church to reintroduce John 4, 9, and 11 in the Sunday Lenten Lectionary as the featured readings for celebrating the Scrutinies. Thus the ancient union between the scrutinies and John's gospel has regained its rightful prominence.

The 1981 Introduction to the *Lectionary for Mass* recommends that, "because these gospels [John 4, 9, and 11] are of major importance in regard to Christian initiation, they may be read in Year B and Year C, especially in places where there are catechumens" (no. 97).[2] That these texts, so long marginalized, should now carry such weight epitomizes the council's vision of Lent through this insistence on baptism as the foundational and unifying Christian sacrament. Read in the baptismal context of Lent, the excerpts from John illustrate what happens when someone meets the risen Lord, and thus provide models through which candidates can interpret their own experience. Proclaimed at key moments in the baptismal retreat of the catechumens, the texts take on special significance: initiation means *passing over* from sin and darkness and death into grace and light and life.

For Years B and C when there are no adult candidates for initiation, the Lectionary provides another set of readings for the Third, Fourth, and

[2]In the event of a community presenting adult candidates for initiation in Years B and C, not only are the Year A gospel passages from John to be read, but the Old Testament readings and the readings from the Apostolic writings for the Third, Fourth, and Fifth Sundays in Year A as well. The three readings for any given Sunday come as an indivisible package.

Fifth Sundays of Lent. In Year B the gospel passages, contrary to the expected pattern, are drawn not from Mark but from John. On the Third Sunday the incident of Jesus overturning the tables of the money changers in the temple (John 2:13-25) is read. In response to the people's challenge, "What sign can you show for doing this?" Jesus answers, "Destroy this temple, and in three days I will raise it up." On the Fourth Sunday the passage presents the second part of Jesus' conversation with Nicodemus, where the Lord points to Moses lifting the bronze serpent in the desert as a sign of his crucifixion (John 3:14-21). In the excerpt for the Fifth Sunday, Jesus explains to the disciples the significance of his death in the parable of the grain of wheat that must die in order to produce fruit (John 12:20-33). In each instance the allusions to Jesus' death and resurrection are obvious. Together these passages emphasize Jesus' coming exaltation, an exaltation that, according to John's gospel, occurs at the hour of his deepest self-abasement—reminders that the paschal mystery always bears the two inseparable facets of cross and resurrection.

In Year C the Lectionary assigns readings from Luke to the Third and Fourth Sundays, and a passage from John to the Fifth. These three readings accentuate the lenten themes of penance and conversion. The word "repent" recurs as a refrain in the Luke 13:1-9 excerpt for the Third Sunday. This is the peculiar episode in which Jesus points to "the Galileans whose blood Pilate had mingled with their sacrifices" and to "those eighteen who were killed when the tower of Siloam fell on them" as warnings to repent and turn to God while there is still time. The well-known parable of the prodigal son is the selection for the Fourth Sunday (Luke 15:1-3, 11-32). Read in Lent Year C, the story of the younger son's return to the father dramatically illustrates the repentance and conversion that lead to renewed life: "for this son of mine was dead and is alive again." Although the passage chosen for the Fifth Sunday comes from John's gospel, scholars today are nearly unanimous in surmising that the episode of the woman caught in adultery (John 8:1-11) was originally a Lucan narrative that inexplicably became inserted in the fourth gospel. The message of repentance and conversion is unmistakable in Jesus' words to the woman, "Go your way, and from now on do not sin again." As a group, these three passages remind the faithful that baptismal commitment, especially for those who were initiated as infants, needs to be continually deepened and reappropriated through repentance and conversion.

The fifteen gospel passages for the first five Sundays of Lent admirably evoke the paschal mystery of Jesus refracted through the particular seasonal themes of baptism and penance. Over the three-year cycle of readings, the Lectionary helps prepare the faithful for Easter by emphasizing major facets of the paschal mystery: the journey through death to new life in baptism (Year A), the self-abasement and exaltation of Jesus as the fundamental pattern of Christian life (Year B), and the continuing appropriation of its significance through penance and conversion (Year C).

Old Testament Readings for the Season of Lent

Sunday	Year A	Year B	Year C
First	Genesis 2:7-9, 16-18, 25; 3:1-7	Genesis 9:8-15	Deuteronomy 26:4-10
Second	Genesis 12:1-4	Genesis 22:1-2, 9-13, 15-18	Genesis 15:5-12, 17-18
Third	Exodus 17:3-7	Exodus 20:1-17	Exodus 3:1-8a, 13-15
Fourth	1 Samuel 16:1b, 6-7, 10-13a	2 Chronicles 36:14-16, 17a, 19-23	Joshua 5:9-12
Fifth	Ezekiel 37:12-14	Jeremiah 31:31-34	Isaiah 43:16-21

The Old Testament selections for Lent display a pattern all their own. According to the 1981 Introduction to the *Lectionary for Mass*, "The Old Testament readings are about the history of salvation, which is one of the themes proper to the catechesis of Lent. The series of texts for each Year presents the main elements of salvation history from its beginning until the promise of the New Covenant" (no. 97).

The texts for the First Sunday of Lent, Years A and B, are selections from what biblical scholars call primeval history, the period stretching from creation (Genesis 1) to the Tower of Babel (Genesis 11). The Year A passage recounts the creation and fall of Adam and Eve. Describing the disobedience that introduced sin and death into the world, this opening act of the biblical story launches the dramatic plot that will find its resolution in the paschal mystery—Jesus, through his obedience, conquered the powers of sin and death. In Year B the excerpt tells of the covenant with Noah and his offspring after the flood. God's attempt to eradicate sin by means of a flood offers a new beginning for humanity. This epic story of the waters of destruction leading to a covenant of blessing prefigures Christian baptism of passage through the waters of death to new life. The excerpt assigned for Year C comes quite surprisingly not from Genesis but from Deuteronomy. It is the text of a confession of faith summarizing God's mighty acts in the early history of Israel, to be recited upon offering the first fruits of the harvest. Although deviating from the Genesis-pattern established in Years A and B, the Lectionary's designers gave this important passage a notable place in the lenten season when candidates confess their new faith for the first time, while the faithful reaffirm it by renewing their baptismal promises. By reaching back to the origins of history, these Old Testament passages suggest that the paschal mystery of Jesus is rooted firmly in the human story and consequently embraces peoples of all times and places.

The Old Testament readings for the Second Sunday of Lent, all of them relating key moments in the story of Abraham, represent the ancestral era. The excerpt from Year A tells of God calling Abraham to be the ancestor of a chosen people through whom all nations will be blessed. In Year B the passage narrates God's covenant with Abraham to grant him numerous offspring and a promised land. The selection for Year C reports the haunting story of Abraham's faith, witnessed in his obeying God's command to sacrifice his beloved son Isaac. The episode prefigures Jesus, the beloved Son of God, who in faith offered himself as a sacrifice for the sins of the world. These stories about the promise of blessing to all nations, about the assurance of a future through numerous offspring, about faithfulness without counting the cost—all find their realization in the paschal mystery of Jesus.

The Lectionary allocates three stories about Moses to the Third Sunday of Lent. Listed chronologically, the Year C excerpt from Exodus 3 relates the well-known burning bush incident, in which God reveals not only the plan to liberate the chosen people from slavery, but also the ineffable name I AM WHO I AM. In the selection from Exodus 17 for Year A, the story of the newly-liberated Hebrew people murmuring against Moses for water in the desert contains overtones of both penance and baptism: penance in the evocation of the forty years of wandering, baptism in the gushing forth of life-giving water. The reading for Year B is the story from Exodus 20 of God's giving the Ten Commandments on Mt. Sinai, a foreshadowing of the feast of Pentecost. This third stage in the Lectionary's lenten sketch of salvation history presents a God who, through mighty deeds and outstretched arm, sets in motion the events assuring that the promised salvation will come to pass.

To the Fourth Sunday of Lent, the Lectionary assigns the theme of the chosen people on their own land. Historically, the first of the events depicted in these selections is recounted in the Year C passage from the

Book of Joshua. The passage describes the first harvest and the first Passover in Canaan, occasions that officially inaugurated Israel's dwelling in the promised land after forty years of wandering in the desert. Next comes the Year A episode from 1 Samuel of the prophet's anointing the shepherd boy David as king of Israel. The story represents the period of the monarchy when the people of God enjoyed freedom as an independent nation and anticipates the New Testament portrayals of Jesus "the Anointed One" (*Messiah* in Hebrew, *Christ* in Greek) and the King of the Jews. The passage from 2 Chronicles for Year B conjures up the spectre of Jerusalem's destruction and the subsequent Babylonian Exile. The passage, however, does not end in hopelessness and despair, for the Lord has "stirred up the spirit of King Cyrus of Persia" who will liberate the people and authorize them to rebuild the temple in Jerusalem. These three readings show that God leads the chosen people, despite their weakness and sinfulness, through the vicissitudes of history toward the promised fulfillment.

The Fifth Sunday is entirely dedicated to prophecies of renewal and restoration proclaimed in the wake of the Babylonian Exile. In Year A the Ezekiel passage expresses the return from exile in the haunting image of the dead coming to life through the power of God's spirit: "I am going to open your graves, O my people; and I will bring you back to the land of Israel." The language of new covenant and of God's law written on the heart phrases Jeremiah's version of the deliverance from exile in the selection for Year B. In Year C Isaiah prophesies that the return to the land of Israel will be like a new Exodus, indeed, a new creation, "I am about to do a new thing," says the Lord. These texts suggest that the human story is being unerringly drawn toward its promised fulfillment in God's future, a hope that, for Christians, is assured in Jesus' resurrection and in his parousia at the end of time.

This five-week *aperçu* of salvation history, structured into each year of the three-year Lectionary cycle, anticipates its more extensive retelling at the Easter vigil. There, only the stage of the people on the land of Israel, the theme for the Fourth Sunday of Lent, has no parallel. While it is true that these Old Testament passages, by virtue of their being proclaimed at the lenten Sunday Eucharists, are read in the light of Christ, they also provide the historical and theological material from which the paschal mystery of Christ gains its depth of meaning. Without the Old Testament, Christian faith would, like a tree without roots, wither away and die.

In addition to these thematic groupings, many Old Testament passages for the Sundays of Lent also correspond with the gospel reading of the day. For example, on the First Sunday of Lent Year A, the reading from Genesis about Adam and Eve's temptation and fall prefigures the story of Jesus' temptation: while our proto-parents succumbed to Satan's wiles, ultimately passing from life to death, Jesus, the last Adam, remains obedient in the face of temptation, in the end passing from death to life. On the Third Sunday of Lent Year A, God's gift of water to the newly-liberated Hebrew people as they wandered in the desert (Exodus 17) foreshadows the story of the Samaritan woman at Jacob's well, to whom Jesus promises the gift of living water "gushing up to eternal life" (John 4). The Fifth Sunday Year A prophecy on the dry bones that are made to live again (Ezekiel 37) anticipates the gospel story of Jesus raising his dead friend Lazarus (John 11). On the Second Sunday Year B, the words of God's command to Abraham, "Take your Son, your only son Isaac, whom you love" (Gen 22:2), are echoed in the gospel's transfiguration scene where God's voice from the cloud addresses the three frightened apostles, "This is my Son, the Beloved; listen to him!" (Mark 9:7). Yet other instances of correspondence between the Old Testament reading and the gospel occur on the Second Sunday of Lent Year B, the Second, Third, and Fifth Sundays Year C. In this way the Lectionary, through its selection and distribution of Old Testament texts, provides stories and images contributing essential threads to the lenten tapestry depicting the paschal mystery of Christ.

Readings from the Apostolic Writings for the Season of Lent

Sunday	Year A	Year B	Year C
First	Romans 5:12-19	1 Peter 3:18-22	Romans 10:8-13
Second	2 Timothy 1:8-10	Romans 8:31-34	Philippians 3:17–4:1
Third	Romans 5:1-2, 5-8	1 Corinthians 1:18, 22-25	1 Corinthians 10:1–6, 10-12
Fourth	Ephesians 5:8-14	Ephesians 2:4-10	2 Corinthians 5:17-21
Fifth	Romans 8:8-11	Hebrews 5:7-9	Philippians 3:8-14

Along with the gospel and the Old Testament readings, the excerpts from the apostolic writings for Lent are also designated according to the principle of harmony. Each selection in its own way, directly or indirectly, and always as refracted through the lenten themes of penance and baptism, proclaims the paschal mystery of Christ. The readings from the apostolic letters during Lent, true to the role of second readings throughout the Sunday and Feast Day Lectionary, interpret the mystery and exhort believers to appropriate it in their lives. Contrary to the gospel and the Old Testament passages for Lent, the second readings lack patterns organized according to thematic groupings.

A perusal of the fifteen readings listed above confirms that the paschal mystery is indeed their primary focus: eleven explicitly mention the death and resurrection of Jesus, while two other passages imply it strongly. The following rapid sampling illustrates the variety of formulations the mystery can assume: ". . . through our Savior Jesus Christ, who abolished death and brought life and immortality to light" (2 Tim 1:10, Second Sunday Year A); ". . . while we were still sinners Christ died for us" (Rom 5:8, Third Sunday Year A); ". . . he was put to death in the flesh, but made alive in the spirit" (1 Pet 3:18, First Sunday Year B); "although he was a Son, he learned obedience through what he suffered" (Heb 5:8, Fifth Sunday Year B); ". . . for our sake God made Christ to be sin who knew no sin, so that in Christ we might become the righteousness of God" (2 Cor 5:21, Fourth Sunday Year C). The repeated use of the first and second person plural pronouns in these readings (seven use "we," four address a plural "you") lend them a strong exhortatory tone. In addition, two passages specifically mention baptism (1 Pet 3:21, First Sunday Year B and 1 Cor 10:2, Third Sunday Year C), and a third implies it (Rom 5:5, Third Sunday Year A). In this way the apostolic authors encourage believers, both then and now, to witness to the paschal mystery in their lives.

In the absence of thematic groupings among the second readings in the Sundays of Lent, correspondence plays as a major role. On each Sunday the selection from the apostolic writings corresponds with either or both of the other readings. Correspondence between the first and second readings can be found, for example, on the Second Sunday of Lent Year A, where God's call to Christians in 2 Timothy 1 echoes the call of Abraham in Genesis 12; on the Second Sunday of Lent Year C, God's pledge in Genesis 15 to give Abraham and his offspring the promised land is transformed in Philippians 3 into the theme of heaven being the true homeland of all believers. Noah and the flood provide the link between the first and second readings for the First Sunday of Lent Year B. On the First Sunday Year C, the confession of faith in Deuteronomy 26 finds an echo in the creed of Romans 10.

The second reading can also correspond with the gospel passage of the day. For instance, on the Fourth Sunday of Lent Year A, the gospel presents Jesus proclaiming that he is the *light* of the world (John 9:5), while the second reading from Ephesians 5:8-14 includes the exhortation, "Live as children of *light.*" A similar correspondence occurs on the Third Sunday of Lent Year B, where in the gospel Jesus' opponents ask for a *sign* justifying his prophetic action in the Temple; in the excerpt from 1 Cor 1:22-25 Paul writes "the Jews demand *signs* . . . but we proclaim Christ crucified." Other cases appear on the Third Sunday Year C, the Fourth Sunday Years B and C, and the Fifth Sunday Year B.

The second reading bridges the first and third readings on the First Sunday of Lent Year A, for example, where Paul's typological comparison between Adam and Christ links the story of Adam's sin in Genesis 3 from the first reading with the gospel story of Jesus' temptation. Other instances appear on the Third and Fifth Sundays Year A, the Second Sunday Year B, and the Fifth Sunday Year C. Thus in their own way the passages from the apostolic writings, as witnesses of early Christian interpretation and appropriation of the paschal mystery, add more threads to the lenten tapestry.

Passion (Palm) Sunday

	Year A	Year B	Year C
Procession	Matthew 21:1-11	Mark 11:1-10	Luke 19:28-40
First reading	Isaiah 50:4-7	same	same
Second reading	Philippians 2:6-11*	same	same
Gospel	Matthew 26:14–27:66*	Mark 14:1–15:47	Luke 22:14–23:56

* readings retained from the *MR* 1570

"The Sixth Sunday, which marks the beginning of Holy Week, is called Passion Sunday (Palm Sunday)" (*GNLYC*, no. 30). In the pre-Vatican II liturgy, the Fifth Sunday of Lent was called Passion Sunday, the Sixth, Palm Sunday. By once again naming the Sixth Sunday of Lent Passion Sunday, the reformed liturgy is reverting to the ancient Roman tradition dating back to the time of St. Leo the Great (d. 461) when the passion (according to Matthew) was read on the Sunday opening Holy Week. It was only in the tenth and eleventh centuries that Rome, via the influence of the Spanish and Gallic Churches, adopted a procession with palms, a tradition stemming from the sixth-century Jerusalem liturgy celebrated on the Sunday before Easter. The current liturgy blends both traditions, with the result that the eucharistic celebration on this day features two gospel readings: the first, proclaimed during the introductory rite, recounts Jesus' triumphal entry into Jerusalem; the second, proclaimed at the usual place in the Liturgy of the Word, relates the passion. Because of the festal character of Passion Sunday, the first and second readings, repeated in all three years of the cycle, are selected according to harmony and correspond with the gospel passion narrative.

As the name indicates, the reading of the passion lends the celebration its special character. The Lectionary distributes the synoptic versions according to the expected pattern, Matthew in Year A, Mark in Year B, and Luke in Year C. As an overture to "The Great Week," as Holy Week was named in the ancient Jerusalem liturgy, the passion touches all the themes that the Easter triduum celebrates more amply and extensively.

The story of Jesus' triumphal entry into the Holy City serves as a prelude to the liturgy of Passion Sunday. Here also the distribution of the synoptic versions follows the usual pattern of Matthew in Year A, Mark in Year B, and Luke in Year C. The juxtaposition of the two gospel passages, one about triumph and the other about passion and crucifixion, announces the themes of the death and resurrection of Jesus' paschal mystery.

The Old Testament reading, Isaiah 50:4-7, is an excerpt from the Third Song of the Suffering Servant, a passage that in the Roman Missal of 1570 was read on Monday of Holy Week. Although the identity of the servant remains a matter of dispute among exegetes, early Christian tradition saw in the four sublime poems (Isa 42:1-4, 49:1-6, 50:4-11, and 52:13–53:12) striking descriptions of Jesus' person and mission. The Third Song's themes of suffering and vindication recommend it for this feast. As the first reading of the day, it sounds the major motifs elaborated in the gospel passion narrative. In addition, the passage forges intimate links with the celebration of the Lord's Passion on Good Friday, where the Lectionary assigns the Fourth Song of the Suffering Servant as the first reading.

In all three Lectionary years, the christological hymn from Philippians (2:5-11) is the selection for the second reading. Its ties with Holy Week are not new, for in the oldest Roman epistolary it accompanied the Passion according to John. One of the most exquisite poetic texts in the New Testament, it tells of Jesus' emptying himself to take on the form of a slave, becoming "obedient to the point of death, even death on a cross." As a result, God exalted him and gave him the name above all other names, the name that until then had been reserved for God alone, that of Lord. Following upon the heels of the Third Song of the Suffering Servant and proclaimed immediately before the passion, it links the two by identifying the servant with Jesus. Together the readings for Passion Sunday conspire to orchestrate a biblically rich overture raising the curtain on the most solemn week of the Church's liturgy.

Conclusion

In contrast to the Great Fifty Days, celebrating the "already" of God's victory over sin and death, the Forty Days observe the "not yet" of its hoped-for fulfillment. If the Easter season adumbrates the Church as the eternal liturgy where the faithful, robed in white, are gathered before the throne of God and of the Lamb, the lenten season underlines the Church as pilgrim, where the faithful, dressed in the sackcloth and ashes of penance, journey through the trials and tribulations of this earthly existence toward the heavenly Jerusalem. Servants are no greater than their master; hence, the Church, composed as it is of disciples of Jesus, must take on the paschal shape of Jesus who suffered and died before being raised. By drawing on a rich trove of biblical stories and images, the Sunday and Feast Day Lectionary plays an essential role in shaping and defining this holy season.

7   The Christmas Season

> Next to the yearly celebration of the paschal mystery, the Church holds most sacred the memorial of Christ's birth and early manifestations. This is the purpose of the Christmas season (no. 32).

> The Christmas season runs from evening prayer I of Christmas until the Sunday after epiphany or after 6 January, inclusive (no. 33).

Thus does the *General Norms for the Liturgical Year and the Calendar* describe and specify the Christmas season. The opening sentence of paragraph 32 appears to say that the Christmas season celebrates something aside from or other than the paschal mystery (*"Next to* the yearly celebration of the paschal mystery . . ."). The qualifying phrase, *"the yearly celebration of the paschal mystery,"* clarifies the document's intent. It indicates that here the term paschal mystery is used in the more restricted meaning of the annual commemoration of the death and resurrection of Jesus at Easter time. However, the Christmas season, like all the seasons that make up the liturgical year, also celebrates the paschal mystery. By transposing it into different modes and keys, this season underscores the mystery's infinite reach and universal embrace. The incarnation, the scandal of the eternal Word of God made flesh and thus becoming subject to all human frailties, even to death itself, reveals the paschal nature of God—the sending of Jesus is God's self-emptying that humankind might be filled with the Spirit of grace and life. To express this sublime mystery, the Christmas season manifests a predilection for the language of darkness and light, the same symbolic threads that embroider the rich tapestry of the Easter vigil.

The Sundays and solemnities that fall between evening prayer I of Christmas (vespers of Christmas eve) until the Sunday after Epiphany or January 6 are the concern of this chapter. These include Christmas with its several Masses (vigil, night, dawn, day), the feast of the Holy Family, the

Solemnity of Mary, Mother of God, the Second Sunday after Christmas, Epiphany, and the Baptism of the Lord.

Principles of Reading Selection and Distribution

For the festal season of Christmas, the Lectionary selects readings according to the principle of harmony—those biblical passages are chosen that best articulate the feasts being celebrated. The prophet Isaiah, from which six of the nine first readings are drawn, stands out as the featured Old Testament book, while the infancy narratives from Matthew 1–2 and Luke 1–2 provide the majority of the gospel pericopes (eight of thirteen), as expected.

Unlike the other liturgical seasons, the Christmas season employs neither thematic groupings nor semicontinuous reading. This is because the Christmas season is constituted primarily of solemnities rather than of Sundays. The two pillars of the season are the feasts of Christmas and Epiphany, the only major feasts of the liturgical calendar that, having escaped the attractive force of Sunday, are celebrated on discrete calendar dates. The other seasonal feasts—Holy Family, Mary the Mother of God, Baptism of the Lord, as well as the Second Sunday after Christmas—are ancillary to the two major ones. Finally, in the absence of thematic groupings and semicontinuous reading, correspondence plays a major role.

Readings for the Christmas Season

The choice of Lectionary readings by and large follows centuries-old Roman tradition. Prescinding from the selections added to fill out the three-year cycle where needed, fully twelve of the sixteen passages from the 1570 Roman Missal reappear in the revised Lectionary, as a glance at the table below shows:

	First reading	Second reading	Gospel
Christmas:			
Vigil	Isaiah 62:1-5	Acts 13:16-17, 22-25	Matthew 1:1-25
Night	Isaiah 9:1-3, 5-6	Titus 2:11-14*	Luke 2:1-14*
Dawn	Isaiah 62:11-12	Titus 3:4-7*	Luke 2:15-20*
Day	Isaiah 52:7-10	Hebrews 1:1-6*	John 1:1-18*

Holy Family A:	Sirach 3:2-6, 12-14	Colossians 3:12-21*	Matthew 2:13-15, 19-23
B:	Genesis 15:1-6; 21:1-3	Hebrews 11:8, 11-12, 17-19	Luke 2:22-40*
C:	1 Samuel 1:20-22, 24-28	1 John 3:1-2, 21-24	Luke 2:41-52*
Mary, Mother of God (January 1)	Numbers 6:22-27	Galatians 4:4-7*	Luke 2:16-21
Second Sunday after Christmas	Sirach 24:1-2,8-10	Ephesians 1:3-6, 15-18	John 1:1-18
Epiphany	Isaiah 60:1-6*	Ephesians 3:2a, 5-6	Matthew 2:1-12*
Baptism of A:	Isaiah 42:1-4, 6-7	Acts 10:34-38	Matthew 3:13-17
the Lord B:	Isaiah 55:1-11	1 John 5:1-9	Mark 1:7-11
C:	Isaiah 40:15, 9-11	Titus 2:11-14; 3:4-7	Luke 3:15-16, 21-22

* readings retained in whole or in part from the *MR* 1570

Because of the peculiar nature of the Christmas season, based as it is on solemnities rather than Sundays, the rationale behind the choice of scripture passages stems from the origins of each feast. That is why in what follows a historical *précis* precedes an examination of the readings assigned.

Christmas

Current scholarship entertains two hypotheses to account for the origin of Christmas. The older and more established view suggests that the feast was instituted in the early fourth, maybe even late third, century by a Church seeking to counter the popularity of the pagan feast of the birth of the Unconquerable Sun, celebrated at the winter solstice. By placing the commemoration of the birth of Jesus at the same time of year, the Church transferred the solstice symbolism of the birth of new light onto Jesus, who Christians believe is the true light that darkness can never overcome.

The second hypothesis complements rather than displaces the first. According to this view, Christians applied to Jesus an ancient Jewish tradition that commemorated the birthdays of illustrious biblical ancestors on the date of their death. Calculated on the Jewish calendar of the day, Jesus died on the fourteenth of Nisan, that is, at Passover, a festival celebrated on the first full moon after the vernal equinox. But instead of commemorating Jesus' birth on the date of his death, Christians celebrated his *conception*, for according to Luke's story of the annunciation the fullness of divinity dwelt in Jesus from the moment of Mary's *fiat*. If Jesus was conceived at Passover time, near the vernal equinox, then he was born nine months later at the winter solstice. The Roman Church celebrates the annunciation on March 25 (the Roman calendar equivalent to the Jewish fourteenth Nisan); hence Jesus' birthday occurred nine months later on December 25.

This computation matches well with other indications in Luke's gospel. Christians conjectured that the priest Zechariah was serving in the temple on the Day of Atonement, roughly at the autumnal equinox, when the angel announced to him the miraculous conception of John the Baptist. At her annunciation, Mary received news that Elizabeth was in her sixth month. Six months after the autumnal equinox means that Mary conceived Jesus at the vernal equinox (March 25). If John the Baptist was conceived at the autumnal equinox, he was born at the summer solstice nine months later. Thus even to this day the liturgical calendar commemorates John's birth on June 24. Finally, John 3:30, where John the Baptist says of Jesus: "He must increase, but I must decrease," corroborates this tallying of dates. For indeed, after the birth of Jesus at the winter solstice the days increase, while after the birth of John at the summer solstice the days decrease.

Both hypotheses explain why the fourth-century Church began to celebrate Jesus' birth at the winter solstice. As a result, the liturgy commemorates the mystery via the symbolism of light—on this day the Sun of Righteousness begins his conquest of the powers of darkness. Light and darkness, therefore, constitute one of the major motifs exploited in the biblical selections for Christmas.

Although Christmas is in fact one feast, the liturgy makes provision for the celebration of four different Masses: at the vigil, in the night, at dawn, and during the day. Beginning in the sixth century, Roman tradition has had the custom of celebrating three Masses at Christmas, a practice first attested in a homily on the nativity preached by Pope Gregory the Great (d. 604). The option of a vigil Mass was added by the Vatican II liturgical reform.

Originally a papal tradition, the celebration of the three Christmas Masses evolved in this way. Popes of the fourth and early fifth centuries customarily celebrated only one Mass on Christmas Day, and this at St.

Peter's Basilica. The addition of a Mass during the night emerged as a result of the growing influence of Jerusalem practices in Rome. In the middle of the fifth century, Roman Christians constructed a replica of the Bethlehem cave where Jesus was born in the new church dedicated to Mary, the Basilica of St. Mary Major. Popular piety led to the celebration there of a Mass at night in imitation of what Christians did in Bethlehem. The third Mass, celebrated at dawn, was originally not related to Christmas. Byzantine authorities living in Rome commemorated the feast of St. Anastasia on December 25. Before going to St. Peter's to celebrate the Christmas Mass during the day, the pope paid his respects to the foreign dignitaries by presiding at the Eucharist in honor of St. Anastasia at the basilica bearing her name. In time, biblical texts about Jesus' birth replaced the original passages read for the saint's commemoration. Thus it became customary for the pope to celebrate three Masses on Christmas. Finally, in the eighth and ninth centuries, when books on the papal liturgy gained favor beyond Rome, the tradition of three Masses at Christmas spread through the rest of Europe.

The gospel passages for the Christmas Masses are constitutive of the feast, for they all have to do in one way or another with the birth of Jesus. At the vigil Eucharist the Lectionary assigns the genealogy from Matthew's gospel. Luke's narrative of the birth of Jesus is proclaimed at Mass in the night, followed by the episode of the adoration of the shepherds at the dawn Mass. Finally, Mass during the day features the prologue from John's gospel, which reaches its high point in the solemn announcement "And the Word became flesh."

Consonant with the underlying solstice symbolism of light overcoming darkness, the Christmas gospels proclaim the birth of Jesus as the dawning of God's promised salvation. At the vigil Mass, the Matthean text recounts how the Lord God revealed to Joseph in a dream that the child whom Mary conceived through the Holy Spirit is to be named Jesus, "for he will save his people from their sins" (Matt 1:21). In the Lucan narrative read during the night, the angel reveals to the frightened shepherds "good news of great joy for all the people"—the birth in the city of David of "a Savior, who is the Messiah, the Lord" (Luke 2:11). The sign confirming the truth of this revelation is "a child wrapped in bands of cloth, lying in a manger," which is precisely what the shepherds, according to the excerpt read at dawn, find awaiting them in Bethlehem (Luke 2:15-20). In the prologue from John for Mass during the day, salvation takes the form of the Word becoming flesh, so that "to all who received him, who believed in his name, he gave power to become children of God" (John 1:12). Matthew's genealogy of Jesus (vigil), Luke's historical introduction contextualizing Jesus' birth (night), and the cosmic language of John's prologue (day) all intimate that the salvation brought about in Jesus embraces peoples of all times and places.

The dawning of salvation characterizes the four Old Testament passages, all drawn from the prophet Isaiah. At the vigil the prophet describes this salvation as light appearing in darkness, as the marriage of heaven and earth, and as a revelation for all peoples. Isaiah 9, read at Mass during the night, prophesies that God's salvation, again clothed in the language of light ("The people who walked in darkness have seen a great light . . .), will be realized in the birth of a child who will establish David's kingdom. In the passage for Mass at dawn, the Lord proclaims "to the end of the earth: 'Say to daughter Zion, See, your salvation comes . . . .'" In the excerpt for Mass during the day, the prophet rhapsodizes, "How beautiful upon the mountains are the feet of the messenger who announces peace, who brings good news, who announces salvation, who says to Zion, 'Your God reigns.'" All of these Isaian oracles speak of Israel's return from the Babylonian Exile. Read at Christmas, they imply that the redemption effected long ago sheds light on the meaning of Jesus' birth: just as God brought the people back to their own land from the darkness of exile, so now in the birth of Jesus God redeems all who believe from the darkness of sin and death.

In each instance there is close correspondence between the Old Testament reading and the gospel passage. At the vigil Mass, God's words addressed to Zion, "For as a young man marries a young woman, so shall your builder marry you, and as the bridegroom rejoices over the bride, so shall your God rejoice over you" (Isa 62:5), foreshadow God's announcement in a dream to Joseph that the child Mary has conceived "is from the Holy Spirit" (Matt 1:18, 20). According to the prophecy read at Mass during the night, the child to be born will "establish and uphold [the throne of David and his kingdom] with justice and with righteousness." In the gospel passage, Luke three times mentions the name David, suggesting that the birth of Jesus realizes the ancient prophecy. In the gospel for Mass at dawn the shepherds find in the child lying in the manger the fulfillment of the angel's words, an announcement echoing the passage from Isaiah where God proclaims to Zion that salvation has come. John's prologue at Mass during the day declares that "the Word became flesh and lived among us" (John 1:14), a fulfillment hinted at in Isaiah's oracle that Zion's sentinels will "lift up their voices" and sing for joy, "for in plain sight they see the return of the Lord to Zion."

While none of the four readings from the apostolic writings speaks of Jesus' birth as such, they all provide interpretations of the event's significance. Each in its own way recapitulates the role of Jesus in God's plan of salvation, usually including a reflection of its impact on those who believe. In the excerpt from Acts 13 read at the Christmas vigil, Paul explains to the assembly in the synagogue at Antioch that Jesus is the awaited Davidic savior: "Of this man's [David's] posterity God has brought to Israel a Savior, Jesus . . . ." The pericope from the Letter to Titus for Mass during the night stresses the effect of Christ's coming. It brings salvation to all, a salvation that already now manifests itself, for it "train[s] us to renounce impiety and worldly passions, and in the present age to live lives that are self-controlled, upright, and godly, while we wait for the manifestation of the glory of our great God and Savior, Jesus Christ." The selection for Mass at dawn, also taken from the Letter to Titus, offers a nutshell summary of salvation history: although humanity in its plight was undeserving, God mercifully sent Jesus to save the world, so that, "having been justified by his grace, we might become heirs according to the hope of eternal life." Finally, at the Mass during the day the Lectionary quotes the opening paragraph of the Letter to the Hebrews. Here Jesus is described as the one through whom everything was created, as "the reflection of God's glory and the exact imprint of God's very being," who made purification for all our sins. All four readings, therefore, proclaim that the coming of Jesus realizes God's plan of salvation and opens the way to its endtime fulfillment when he will come again in glory.

The second readings for Christmas correspond with either or both of the other readings. At the vigil Mass, Paul's sketch of the history of Israel finds a counterpart in the gospel genealogy of Jesus, with both texts singling out Jesus' Davidic ascendency. The excerpt from Titus for Mass during the night announces that "the grace of God has appeared, bringing salvation to all," echoing the prophetic proclamation "the people who walked in darkness have seen a great light." The salvation foreseen in the first reading for Mass at dawn ("See your salvation comes" [Isa 62:11]) comes to pass in the advent of Jesus: "When the goodness and loving kindness of God our Savior appeared, he saved us" (Titus 3:4). Hebrews 1:1-6 for Mass during the day offers a felicitous correspondence with John's prologue. Paired with the evangelist's "the Word was God . . . the Word became flesh" are such phrases from Hebrews as "God . . . has spoken to us by a Son . . . (who) is the reflection of God's glory and the exact imprint of God's very being."

The twelve scripture readings for Christmas provide a "treasure-house of images"[1] articulating the revelation of the mystery hidden long ago, that from all time God had planned to save the world under the yoke of sin and death through the sending of the Son. The birth of Jesus sheds light upon a darkened world, unites heaven and earth, and opens the way to the fullness of life. Christmas celebrates God's pledge that, as surely as the Word became flesh, "emptying himself, taking the form of a slave, being born in human likeness," God continues to embrace humankind enslaved by darkness and sin, leading all people of good will to fullness of life and light.

Epiphany

In many ways Epiphany is the Eastern Christian counterpart to Christmas. Like Christmas, the origins of Epiphany can be traced to a combination of calendrical computation and Christianization of pagan feasts. Unlike Christmas, however, Epiphany celebrated not only Jesus' birth but his other early manifestations as well. Later, Rome adopted the Eastern feast and adapted it to its already well-developed Christmastide by focusing only on Jesus' manifestation to the Gentiles.

The feast is based on the old Egyptian calendar which celebrated the winter solstice on January 6. The calendrical computation approach, applying the Jewish tradition of celebrating the birth (here, the conception) of an illustrious biblical figure on the date of his or her death, placed Jesus' crucifixion on April 6, the Egyptian calendar equivalent to the fourteenth Nisan. If Jesus was conceived on that date, he was born nine months later on January 6. The celebration of Jesus' birth, however, accommodating influences from gnosticism and surrounding pagan customs, also took on baptismal overtones. According to an ancient Gnostic sect, divinity began to dwell in Jesus not at his conception but at his baptism, a point of view based on the fact that Mark's gospel, which has no infancy narratives, begins its version of the story of Jesus with his baptism by John in the Jordan. At the same time, two pagan feasts, both celebrated on January 6—the commemoration of the birth of Aion, god of time and eternity, and the festival of drawing water from the Nile, the annual rebirth of the life-source for the Egyptians—contributed further light and water symbolism to the Christian feast.

A final influence on the shape and content of the feast comes from the New Testament. The word *epipháneia* (Greek for manifestation) origi-

---

[1] The phrase is Gerard Sloyan's, from his article "A Treasure-House of Images," *Liturgy 90* 21 (August-September 1990) 7–9, 15.

nally denoted the official state visit of a king or an emperor, especially "on occasions when he publicly showed himself to the people."[2] By extension it was applied to the appearance of a god, or again to a god's intervention in human affairs. While the New Testament employs the noun in most instances to describe the manifestation of the risen Christ in his Parousia at the end of time (see 2 Thess 2:8; 1 Tim 6:14; 2 Tim 1:10; 4:1, 8; Titus 2:13), it uses the cognate verb *phanerô* to express God, but more especially Jesus, *revealing* his glory. John 2:11, for example, concludes the episode of Jesus changing water into wine at Cana in this way: "Jesus did this, the first of his signs, in Cana of Galilee, and *revealed* his glory." Other similar occurrences appear in John 1:31; 3:21; 7:4; 9:3; 17:6; and 21:1, 14. Over the centuries, the various strands merged with the result that Epiphany eventually celebrated not only Jesus' first manifestation as a human being (his birth), but also his first manifestation to the Jewish people (in the guise of the shepherds at Bethlehem), his first manifestation to the Gentiles (represented by the Magi), the first manifestation of the Trinity (at Jesus' baptism, where God's voice is heard and the Spirit descends in the form of a dove), and his first manifestation to his disciples (at the miracle at Cana).

Epiphany came to Rome via the circuitous route of Spain and Gaul, where its baptismal aspects, very much in keeping with its Eastern origins, emerged as dominant. Unlike the Roman tradition which interpreted baptism as a dying and rising with Christ (hence its gravitation toward Eastertide), the Eastern tradition transplanted in Western Europe saw baptism more as a rebirth, an illumination, a manifestation of God's life in our own. Once the feast reached Rome, it underwent some modifications. Rome already had December 25 to commemorate Jesus' birth and the Easter vigil to celebrate the baptism of new members. Thus the Roman Church incorporated the feast, but restricted the focus to the visit of the Magi, Jesus' first manifestation to the Gentiles.

The other facets of Epiphany are not lost, however. Today's revised Roman calendar celebrates other manifestations of Jesus' divinity on the Sundays following January 6—the baptism of Jesus falls on the Sunday after January 6, the miracle at Cana appears on the Second Sunday in Ordinary Time, Year C. Whereas in the Eastern tradition Epiphany is a "layered" feast celebrating the many manifestations of Jesus stacked together on one calendar date, the Roman tradition unpacks the feast, distributing the commemoration of Jesus' manifestations over several celebrations.

[2]Francis X. Weiser, *Handbook of Christian Feasts and Customs. The Year of the Lord in Liturgy and Folklore* (New York: Harcourt, Brace, and Co., 1958 [1952]) 141.

As for the scriptural readings, the 1981 Introduction to the *Lectionary for Mass* offers the following summary: "On Epiphany, the Old Testament reading and the gospel continue the Roman tradition; the text for the reading from the apostolic letters is about the calling of all peoples to salvation" (no. 95). The gospel reading for Epiphany from Matthew 2, the visit of the Magi, is constitutive of the feast. This familiar, beloved story is a mini-gospel foreshadowing the future destiny of the infant Jesus. Just as Herod sought the life of the child, the religious and political authorities will one day succeed in putting Jesus to death; just as the Magi came from afar to worship the infant, the crucified and risen Christ will draw all peoples to himself. The Magi's gifts also betoken the baby's fate. Myrrh, an aromatic substance derived from various shrubs and trees, conjures up Jesus' death (in Mark 15:23, Jesus on the cross is offered wine mingled with myrrh) and burial (in John 19:39, Nicodemus brought myrrh and aloes for Jesus' burial). Frankincense is a fragrant gum resin producing a pleasant odor when burned. Traditionally offered only to God at the temple in Jerusalem, its use here points to Jesus' divine status. Gold, the regal element evoking immortality because it does not tarnish, symbolizes the glory of the risen Christ reigning as Lord at God's right hand.

Gold and frankincense, specifically mentioned in the last verse of the Old Testament selection, are not the only features recommending Isaiah 60:1-6 as first reading. The prophet's vision of nations and treasure-bearing kings streaming to a radiant, restored Zion where the Lord will once again make the light of his glory dwell strikes the chords of all the major epiphany motifs. Ephesians 3:2-3a, 5-6 is a worthy substitute for the traditional Roman Missal passage from Titus 2:11-14, which is now assigned to the Christmas Mass at night. If in the Isaian prophecy Gentiles come to Zion to "proclaim the praise of the Lord," in Ephesians the Gentiles "have become fellow heirs, members of the same body, and sharers in the promise in Christ Jesus through the gospel." This is the great mystery that "in former generations . . . was not made known to humanity as it has now been revealed to [God's] holy apostles and prophets by the Spirit."

In the feast of Epiphany, the Church celebrates the dawn of God's salvation, which first appeared in the birth of Jesus, reaching to the ends of the earth and dispelling the darkness of night for all peoples.

Other Major Celebrations of the Christmas Season

The ancillary feasts of the Holy Family; Solemnity of Mary, Mother of God, Second Sunday after Christmas; and Baptism of the Lord enrich the Church's liturgy by reflecting different facets of Christ's birth and early manifestations. As with the pillar feasts of Christmas and Epiphany, history informs current usage.

Feast of the Holy Family (Sunday within the Octave of Christmas)

The Feast of the Holy Family is the most recent, and as a result perhaps the least integrated, addition to the Christmas season. What has now become a liturgical celebration began as popular devotion. The first evidence of devotional groups dedicated to the theme of Jesus, Mary, and Joseph in their domestic life at Nazareth as a model for Catholic families appears in seventeenth-century Europe and French-speaking Canada. In the nineteenth century the growing secularization of marriage and family life led to a surge in the devotion's popularity. To support the pious associations dedicated to shoring up the threatened values of marriage and family, Pope Leo XIII instituted the feast of the Holy Family on June 14, 1893, and placed it as an optional feast on the Third Sunday after Epiphany.

In 1914 Pope Benedict XV transferred the feast to the fixed date of January 19. But this had the unfortunate effect of removing it from the Sunday calendar. On October 26, 1921, the same pope remedied the situation by moving the feast once again, this time to the First Sunday after Epiphany, proclaiming it an obligatory feast for the universal Church. It was this new location on the liturgical calendar that led to the connection with Christmas, albeit in a somewhat indirect way. In the Roman Missal of 1570, the gospel passage for the First Sunday after Epiphany was the Lucan episode of the boy Jesus teaching the elders in the temple (Luke 2:42-52). Since the story is part of the infancy narratives, the feast became identified with stories of Jesus' birth. It was but a small step to incorporate it into the Christmas cycle where the two first chapters of Luke's gospel feature so highly. That is precisely what the Vatican II revision did. The members of *Coetus I*, the *Consilium* committee for the revision of the liturgical calendar, placed the feast where it now stands, on the Sunday within the Octave of Christmas.

Locating the Feast of the Holy Family between Christmas and Epiphany demonstrates once again the liturgy's unconcern for linearity. In Year A the gospel passage relates the *sequel* to the Magi's visit, while the pericope recounting the visit itself, read only on January 6, is still more than a week away. The same goes for Year C. The gospel for the Holy Family presents the *twelve-year-old boy* Jesus teaching in the Temple, an episode read before the Epiphany story of the Magi adoring the *infant*

Jesus. A concern for biographically-based chronology would logically have placed these texts between Epiphany and the Baptism of Jesus. However, the calendar committee's decision to respect the ancient sequence of the three manifestations of Jesus—Epiphany, Baptism, Cana (now Second Sunday in Ordinary Time, Year C)—precluded such a solution. The chronology of Jesus' life has never been the primary concern of the liturgy, which provides insight into mystery, not a narrative of events.

The feast provides an opportunity to read passages from the infancy narratives that might otherwise not appear at all in the Sunday and Feast Day Lectionary. Indeed, the scriptural selections for the Holy Family offer an especially rich treasure of images. The gospel passages for the Holy Family were selected because they all speak of Joseph, Mary, and Jesus. The flight into Egypt (Matthew 2:13-15, 19-23, Year A), the elderly prophets Simeon and Anna at the presentation in the Temple (Luke 2:22-40, Year B), and the finding of the boy Jesus in the Temple (Luke 2:41-52, Year C)—stories solidly implanted in Christian imagination—are filled with foreshadowings. In the first, Herod's seeking to kill the infant prefigures Jesus' arrest, trial, and crucifixion. Simeon's foreboding words to Mary, that her child "is destined for the falling and the rising of many in Israel," presage the struggles Jesus' message will engender. The twelve-year-old Jesus teaching in the Temple with wisdom and authority signals his public ministry of preaching and teaching the good news. Thus, while presenting Christmas-related tableaus of Jesus' infancy and childhood, these gospel stories encompass wider aspects of the paschal mystery of Christ.

The 1969 edition of the Lectionary assigned the same Old Testament passage and excerpt from the apostolic writings to all three years of the cycle. The 1981 edition has now added first readings and second readings for Years B and C. The Old Testament readings for the feast, selected according to the principle of harmony, all have to do with parents and children. In Year A, the wise man Jesus, son of Sirach, exhorts children to obey, honor, and respect their parents. The wonderful narrative of God making good on the promise to provide a son to the elderly couple Abraham and Sarah is read in Year B. The story of childless Hannah, who through God's favor becomes the mother of the prophet Samuel, graces Year C. As to correspondence between the Old Testament and the gospel, in Year B two sets of elderly people, Abraham and Sarah, Simeon and Anna, rejoice in the birth of a child who embodies God's promise. In Year C the reading from 1 Samuel corresponds with the Lucan gospel passage: Hannah dedicates her son Samuel to serve in "the *house of the Lord* at Shiloh"; Jesus, in the Temple among the elders, responds to his anxious parents, "Why were you searching for me? Did you not know that I must be in *my Father's house?*"

The readings from the apostolic writings reflect the main themes of the feast, expressed for the most part in the form of exhortation. The Year A Colossians text about family life in the Lord echoes the first reading from Sirach. In Year B, the excerpt from the Letter to the Hebrews praises Abraham and Sarah's faith in God who, as evidenced in the birth of Isaac to an elderly couple beyond child-bearing age, "is able even to raise someone from the dead." The pericope from 1 John also speaks about children: "See what love the Father has given us, that we should be called children of God; and that is what we are." Just as in the first and third readings Samuel and Jesus are dedicated to the service of God, so also Christians serve the Father when they "believe in the name of his Son Jesus Christ and love one another, just as he has commanded. . . ."

Although the gospels provide virtually no information on the domestic life of Jesus, Mary, and Joseph in Nazareth, the Lectionary for the Feast of the Holy Family has pieced together a rich assembly of biblical passages enhancing the Church's celebration of the Christmas season. In being made flesh, the Word of God emptied himself of his "equality with God" (Phil 2:6) to share with humankind the humble reality of family life.

Solemnity of Mary, Mother of God

The Octave of Christmas has had a very interesting and eventful history. By giving priority to the motherhood of Mary on this eighth day after Christmas, the Vatican II reform of the liturgy has returned to one of the most venerable traditions in Christian liturgy.

The feast of Mary, Mother of God originated in the East. On December 26 the Eastern Churches celebrated (and still celebrate today) the feast of the Congratulation of Mary in commemoration of her role in salvation history as Mother of God. In the fifth century the Roman Church adopted the feast (the first Marian feast in the West), but placed it on January 1 to counter the influence of pagan celebrations of the New Year.

In the sixth and seventh centuries Churches in Spain and Gaul celebrated the circumcision of Jesus on the Octave of Christmas, in accordance with Luke 2:21: "After eight days had passed, it was time to circumcise the child." This tradition reached Rome in the twelfth century, and from that time until the reform of Vatican II, the feast of Mary, Mother of God ceded the spotlight to the commemoration of the circumcision of Jesus.

Yet another theme, that of the Holy Name, gravitated within the orbit of the Octave of Christmas. Primarily identified with Bernard of

Citeaux who promoted the devotion in the twelfth century, it was officially approved for Franciscans in 1530 by Pope Clement VII. Other religious orders adopted the devotion, leading Pope Innocent XIII in 1721 to institute a feast of the Holy Name for the entire Church, which he placed on the Second Sunday after Epiphany. In 1913 Pius X moved it to the Sunday between January 2 and 5, that is, as close as possible to the octave, for in Jewish tradition the name of the child was given on the day of his circumcision, as attested in Luke 2:21: "After eight days had passed, it was time to circumcise the child; and he was called Jesus, the name given by the angel before he was conceived in the womb."

The Vatican II reform abolished the special feast of the Holy Name and reinstituted the commemoration of Mary on the Octave of Christmas in place of the circumcision. However, the traditional composite nature of this feast can still be discerned in the gospel selection of the day. The primary theme of Mary, Mother of God appears clearly in the gospel passage that highlights Mary's response to the wondrous birth of her son Jesus: "Mary treasured all these words and pondered them in her heart" (Luke 2:19). The same pericope goes on to include a passing mention of the other two traditional themes, circumcision and holy name: "After eight days had passed, it was time to circumcise the child; and he was called Jesus . . ." (Luke 2:21).

The Marian focus is conspicuously underlined in the second reading from Paul's Letter to the Galatians. It is the earliest mention of Mary in the entire New Testament (Paul wrote the letter in the early 50s, some two decades before the earliest gospel), as well as the only passage where the Apostle alludes to Jesus' mother. On two counts the excerpt corresponds with the gospel of the day. Jesus, writes Paul, was "born of woman, born under the law" (Gal 4:4). The first is obvious, for the unnamed woman in Galatians is Mary, the mother of Jesus. Second, by undergoing circumcision on the eighth day after his birth, Jesus gives evidence of having been "born under the law."

The Old Testament passage is the beautiful and oft-quoted Aaronic blessing:

> The Lord bless you and keep you;
> the Lord make his face to shine upon you,
> and be gracious to you;
> the Lord lift up his countenance upon you,
> and give you peace. (Num 6:24-26)

This is a splendid prayer for New Year's Day, when in many cultures parents bless their children. The main reason for selecting the text, however, lies in the verse immediately following the blessing, where God enjoins Moses: "So shall they [Aaron and his sons] put my name on the Israelites, and I will bless them." Just as in the Old Testament the people of Israel were to be blessed in the name of God, those who choose to follow the newborn Son of God will find blessing in the name of Jesus, which means "God saves."

This ancient feast, rightly restored to an eminent place in the Christmas season, lends a special aura to the Church's liturgical year by unfolding further the implications of the incarnation—Jesus is at one and the same time Son of God and Son of Mary, both divine and human. Perhaps more than the other feasts of this holy season, the Solemnity of Mary, Mother of God best articulates the profound joy expressed in the Christmas solemn blessing: "When the Word became man, earth was joined to heaven." That the *Exsultet* should use similar words to proclaim Christ's resurrection at the Easter vigil ("night truly blessed, when heaven is wedded to earth . . .") simply points out once again how the paschal mystery permeates every aspect of the Church's liturgy.

Second Sunday after Christmas

According to the *GNLYC*, "the Sunday falling between 2 January and 5 January is the Second Sunday after Christmas" (no. 36). Already a Sunday without a special commemoration, it is further eclipsed in those countries where Epiphany, having lost its status as a holy day of obligation, is no longer celebrated on January 6, but is assigned "to the Sunday occurring between 2 January and 8 January" (no. 37). Thus the Second Sunday after Christmas is a filler whose themes are drawn from its proximity to the pillar feasts of Christmas and Epiphany.

The scriptural passages, the same for all three years of the cycle, are selected according to harmony so as to express the main themes of the Christmas season. Although this Sunday's liturgical status pales in the light of the feasts that surround it, the readings are resplendent with theological insight and significance. The gospel text from John 1:1-18, repeated here from the Christmas Mass during the day, assures that the faithful who attended any of the three other Christmas Masses might still have the opportunity to hear this magnificent passage. There is no more profound and felicitous way of expressing the mystery of the incarnation than in the words from the prologue of John's gospel: "In the beginning was the Word . . . And the Word became flesh and lived among us."

In correspondence with the theme of God dwelling in our midst, the Old Testament selection from Sirach portrays Wisdom, created "from

eternity," pitching her tent in Israel, an image which the earliest generations of Christians interpreted as foreshadowing the coming of the Word
of God, who in his incarnation came to live among us. The passage from
Ephesians praises God who "chose us in Christ before the foundation of
the world to be holy and blameless before him in love." The gospel phrase
"In the beginning was the Word," witnessing that God's plan of salvation
has existed from all time, echoes Wisdom in the first reading, who was
created "before the ages, in the beginning." Together these texts imply that
the mystery of the incarnation is not a last minute, ad hoc decision. It is
the revelation of God's love at work from all eternity.

Baptism of the Lord

Originally commemorated on the octave of Epiphany (January 13),
the Baptism of the Lord now appears on "the Sunday falling after January
6" (*GNLYC*, no. 38). Liturgically the feast serves two purposes. As a commemoration of one of the manifestations of Jesus, it closes the Christmas
season. As the inauguration of Jesus' public ministry, the Baptism of the
Lord opens the season of Ordinary Time.

The gospel excerpts are drawn from the synoptic accounts of Jesus'
baptism, Matthew's in Year A, Mark's in Year B, and Luke's in Year C. All
three versions recount the same essential aspects of the event. Jesus, by
submitting to John's baptism of repentance in a gesture of solidarity with
humankind, is proclaimed beloved Son by God's voice thundering from
the heavens, and receives the Holy Spirit which descends upon him in the
form of a dove. Thus Jesus' baptism formally identifies him and equips
him with the divine power to embark on his mission of preaching the
good news of God's kingdom.

While the first edition of the Lectionary offered the same Old
Testament reading and excerpt from the apostolic writings for all three
years of the cycle, the 1981 edition now provides first and second readings
for Years B and C as well. Interestingly, these added passages already appear elsewhere in the Sunday and Feast Day Lectionary.[3] The Old
Testament passage from Isaiah in Year A, an excerpt from the first of the
four Songs of the Suffering Servant, corresponds well with the voice from

---

[3]The Year B selection from Isaiah 55 is read on all three years at the Easter vigil; the
excerpt from Isaiah 40 for Year C occurs on the Second Sunday of Advent Year B; most of
1 John 5:1-9 for Year B is also assigned to the Second Sunday of Easter Year B; and the first
part of Year C's Titus passage, 2:11-14, appears as the second reading for the Christmas
Mass during the night, the second part, 3:4-7, for the Christmas Mass at dawn.

heaven in the gospel: in both cases God names a chosen one and confers upon him a special mission.[4] The Old Testament reading for Year B commends itself on this feast for the number of themes it touches upon. Not only does the passage mention water ("come to the waters," v. 1; "for as the rain and snow come down from heaven," v. 10a), it also speaks of David as a special witness to the peoples (v. 4), calls Israel to repentance (v. 7), and proclaims the efficaciousness of God's word (vv. 10-11). All these aspects can be applied to Jesus' baptism as well as to that of Christians throughout the ages. The baptismal interpretation of this passage from Isaiah is further underlined by its use at the Easter vigil, the baptismal moment *par excellence*. The passage from Isa 40:1-5, 9-11 for Year C speaks of the revelation of God's glory. Paired with Luke's account of Jesus' baptism, this Isaiah proclamation takes on new Christic overtones, for in Jesus the promise that "all flesh will see the glory of the Lord" is fulfilled.

The reading for Year A from the apostolic writings is drawn from the only passage in the Acts of the Apostles that mentions Jesus' baptism. In his speech at Cornelius' house, Peter explains that in the baptism "God anointed Jesus of Nazareth with the Holy Spirit and with power" (Acts 10:38). This passage, read on Easter Sunday as well, corresponds with both the gospel and the first reading. For Year B the suggested second reading comes from the First Letter of John, where Jesus is described as "the one who came by water and blood" (1 John 5:6). Moreover, God testifies on Jesus' behalf through the three witnesses of "the Spirit and the water and the blood" (1 John 5:7), echoing the themes of water and spirit in the gospel pericope. In Year C the Lectionary proposes a composite passage from the Letter to Titus (2:11-14 and 3:4-7). The text explicitly mentions that believers are saved "through the water of rebirth and renewal by the Holy Spirit" (3:5). The passages for Years B and C exhort believers to live their lives in a holiness worthy of their baptismal calling.

The promise and anticipation generated by Jesus' birth begin to be realized in his baptism, the first act of his public ministry, a baptism that contains the hidden seed of the paschal mystery. For the Lord himself later confronts his disciples with the ominous words, "Are you able to drink the cup that I drink, or be baptized with the baptism that I am baptized with?" (Mark 10:38).

[4]It is worth noting that all four Songs of the Suffering Servant appear in the Sunday Lectionary: the first (Isa 42:1-4, 6-7) on the Baptism of Jesus; the second (Isa 49:1-6) on the Second Sunday in Ordinary Time Year A, where it is paired with John's version of the baptism of Jesus (John 1:29-34); the third (Isa 50:4-11) on Passion Sunday; and the fourth (Isa 52:13–53:12) on Good Friday.

Conclusion

Although lacking the studied architecture manifested elsewhere in the liturgical year, the Christmas season nevertheless rests solidly on the pillars of the two ancient feasts of Christmas and Epiphany. For this season as for the others, the Lectionary proves itself equal to the task of selecting a rich array of passages to enhance the Church's liturgical celebration of the mystery hidden long ago, but now revealed to all flesh—God's salvation has dawned in the birth of Jesus, the light of the world.

8   The Season of Advent

The following description of Advent from the *GNLYC* succinctly captures the gist of the season:

> Advent has a twofold character: as a season to prepare for Christmas when Christ's first coming to us is remembered; as a season when that remembrance directs the mind and heart to await Christ's Second Coming at the end of time. Advent is thus a period for devout and joyful expectation (no. 39).

Behind this straightforward definition, however, lies a long and often ambiguous history that leads one commentator to declare: "Advent presents more problems than any other season in the liturgical year. Not the least of these problems is that of knowing how to observe the season."[1] A perusal of the origins and development of Advent offers some help, even if the results are not entirely unequivocal.

Advent first appeared in Spain and Gaul where, as far back as the fourth and fifth centuries, there is evidence of a three-week period of penitential practices in preparation for Christmas and Epiphany. Whether it was originally designed as a preparation for baptism at Epiphany remains disputed. In any event, prayer, fasting, and more frequent attendance at church, particularly from December 17 through to Epiphany (to offset the influence of the pagan Saturnalia?) characterized the season. In time this period of preparation for Christmas and Epiphany took on many of the penitential trappings of Lent. Extended to four, in some instances even six, weeks, Advent featured fasting three days a week, the use of the liturgical color purple signifying repentance, and forgoing the *Gloria* and the *Alleluia* in eucharistic celebrations. However, whereas the lenten penitential practices drew their inspiration from reflection on Jesus' passion and

---

[1] J. Neil Alexander, "Advent, Christmas and Epiphany," *Liturgy* 4/3 (1984) 9.

death, Advent turned to the Lord's second coming as judge of the living and the dead to impress upon Christians the need for conversion.

During the same period, Advent in Rome took on a different flavor. Instead of a penitential preparation in expectation of the second coming, the Roman Church elaborated a four-week liturgical preparation aimed at commemorating the birth of Jesus at Christmas. By the seventh century, Gallic and Spanish traditions began to make inroads in Rome, thus giving the season a double orientation—preparation for Christ's first coming at his birth and anticipation of his second coming at the end of time—celebrated through a blend of liturgical and penitential observances.

Two further considerations influenced the eschatological orientation of the season. The first has to do with the Vulgate, the standard Latin version of the scriptures in the West, the second with changes in the liturgical calendar. The Vulgate used the word *adventus*, which simply means coming, to translate *parousía*—the word nearly always employed in the Greek New Testament to designate Christ's second coming (see Matt 24:3, 27, 37, 39; 1 Cor 15:23; 2 Thess 2:8). Thus the word *adventus*, from which is derived Advent, came to evoke first and foremost, not just any coming, but the endtime return of the Lord as judge. Calendar changes also left their imprint on the season. In the early Middle Ages the liturgical year began on December 24. The last weeks of the liturgical year, the weeks immediately preceding Christmas vigil, featured biblical passages about Christ's second coming at the end of time. When in the ninth century the beginning of the liturgical year was transferred to the First Sunday of Advent, the last weeks of the liturgical year with their eschatological readings became part of Advent.

Although Advent in the post-Vatican II liturgy still uses the color purple and drops the *Gloria* (but not the *Alleluia*) from eucharistic celebrations, it has set aside the penitential practices long identified with the season. Instead, as evidenced in the *GNLYC*, Advent now celebrates the two traditional themes of commemoration of Christ's first coming at Christmas and anticipation of his second coming at the end of time. The two aspects complement each other, as Adolf Adam explains: "For the incarnation as a historical event marks the beginning of our salvation and ensures its completion in the return of Christ."[2] Because Jesus emptied himself by taking on human form, "becoming obedient to the point of death—even death on a cross" (Phil 2:8), God highly exalted him and

---

[2]Adolf Adam, *The Liturgical Year: Its History and Its Meaning after the Reform of the Liturgy,* trans. Matthew J. O'Connell (New York: Pueblo, 1981) 131.

made him the Lord of all creation. Between his first and second comings, this risen Christ is not idle, however. As Lord reigning at God's right hand, he is at work shaping and molding all things into the pattern of his paschal mystery. Thus the Sundays in Advent, while commemorating his birth and anticipating his return, celebrate in word and sacrament his coming now in the midst of this world.

Like the winter solstice feast of Christmas for which it is a preparation, Advent articulates the paschal mystery in the seasonal images of light and darkness. The use of such primordial and pervasive symbols here suggests the cosmic and universal reach of Christ's death and resurrection. Wherever and however they happen, all transformations from darkness to light are, in the eyes of faith, the working out of the paschal mystery in the world until it achieves its completion at the Lord's second coming.

Principles of Reading Selection and Distribution

As is the case for all festal seasons, the Lectionary selects readings for Advent according to the principle of harmony: passages are chosen in function of the season's main themes. The 1981 Introduction to the *Lectionary for Mass* specifies how the scriptural passages are distributed:

> Each gospel reading has a distinctive theme: the Lord's coming at the end of time (First Sunday of Advent), John the Baptist (Second and Third Sunday), and the events that prepared immediately for the Lord's birth (Fourth Sunday).
>
> The Old Testament readings are prophecies about the Messiah and the Messianic age, especially from Isaiah.
>
> The readings from an apostle serve as exhortations and as proclamations, in keeping with the different themes of Advent (no. 93).

Accordingly, the Advent selections exhibit thematic groupings and correspondence, but no semicontinuous reading.

Beyond these clearly discernible patterns, the selection and distribution of Sunday readings are also indirectly influenced by the weekday pattern of readings. Advent falls into two parts: the first encompasses the beginning until December 16; the second stretches from December 17 to 24. The first part stresses the eschatological aspect, while the second part focuses more immediately on the upcoming commemoration of Jesus' birth. The Sunday readings reflect this, where only the Fourth Sunday of Advent, which always falls between December 17 and 24, anticipates the birth of Jesus.

Gospel Readings for Advent

Sunday	Year A	Year B	Year C
First	Matthew 24:37-44	Mark 13:33-37	Luke 21:25-28, 34-36*
Second	Matthew 3:1-12	Mark 1:1-8	Luke 3:1-6
Third	Matthew 11:2-11*	John 1:6-8, 19-28*	Luke 3:10-18
Fourth	Matthew 1:18-24	Luke 1:26-38	Luke 1:39-45*
	* readings retained from the *MR* 1570.		

A cursory glance at the above table shows that, except for the Third and Fourth Sundays of Advent in Year B, the Lectionary respects the usual pattern of assigning excerpts from Matthew to Year A, Mark to Year B, and Luke to Year C. Each Sunday celebrates a particular aspect of the season. Drawn from Jesus' last discourse before his arrest, the passages for the First Sunday of Advent, replete with terrifying images of the final judgment, tell of the Son of Man's return at the end of time to establish God's kingdom in fullness. On the Second Sunday, John the Baptist proposes the kind of activity and behavior believers are to adopt in preparation for the coming of the kingdom. The texts of the Third Sunday introduce Jesus, the person through whom the kingdom will be inaugurated, while those of the Fourth Sunday announce how his birth is to take place.

Despite their disconcerting descriptions of the cataclysmic end of the world, the gospel excerpts for the First Sunday of Advent are intended to reassure the faithful that God's promised salvation will indeed come to pass. It is not a question of *if*, but merely of *when*, the Son of Man will return in glory—the event is certain, only the hour of its occurrence is unknown. What was begun in a humble, hidden way in Bethlehem will be made manifest in all its splendor at the end of time. Through the paschal mystery of Jesus, this imperfect world, travailing under the burden of sin and death, will one day be liberated and transformed. With this assurance in mind, disciples are to remain alert and vigilant, calm and sober, giving in neither to despair nor to frenzied activism, keeping hope burning brightly through prayer and purposeful action. In this way the gospel excerpts for the First Sunday set the fundamental tone for Advent as "a period for devout and joyful expectation" (*GNLYC*, no. 39).

The figure of John the Baptist dominates the gospel passages for the Second and Third Sundays of Advent. Each of the three Lectionary years stresses different aspects of the same basic message: John announces that, through the agency of "one more powerful than I . . . who will baptize you with Holy Spirit and fire," God is about to realize the promises made long ago; be prepared! On the Second Sunday of Advent Year A, John is portrayed as the long-awaited Elijah figure who has returned to usher in the Day of the Lord. His fiery preaching intends to lead the crowds to a baptism of repentance. The excerpt for the Third Sunday presents Jesus explaining how in his ministry the prophetic signs of God's salvation are being realized: "The blind receive their sight, the lame walk, the lepers are cleansed, the deaf hear, the dead are raised, and the poor have good news preached to them."

In Year B the Lectionary selects the opening of Mark's gospel for the Second Sunday of Advent. Here, John's preaching is more succinctly reported than in Matthew's version, but the message is the same—the Day of the Lord is at hand, repent and believe. Because Mark's gospel has less material on John the Baptist than Matthew's and Luke's, and in order to honor an ancient tradition preserved by the Roman Missal of 1570, the Lectionary turns to John's gospel for the Third Sunday of Advent Year B. The passage combines the two paragraphs from chapter one in which John the Baptist witnesses to the Word made flesh: "Among you stands one whom you do not know, the one who is coming after me."

In Year C the Lucan selection for the Second Sunday provides the historical context for John's appearance and extends the Isaiah citation to emphasize the universal reach of God's action in Christ: ". . . and all flesh shall see the salvation of God." The Third Sunday features elements from John's preaching unique to the third gospel. Translating repentance into tangible actions, John urges the crowds to share with the needy, the tax collectors to "collect no more than the amount prescribed," the soldiers not to extort money and to "be satisfied with your wages." Although John's preaching, contained in these six passages distributed over the three-year cycle of the Second and Third Sundays of Advent, originally prepared for the coming of Jesus two millennia ago, the Baptist's message is just as apposite for believers today who yearn for fulfillment of all things at Jesus' second coming.

The gospel selections for the Fourth Sunday of Advent relate the familiar story of Jesus' conception and of Mary's visitation. In Year A Matthew narrates how in a dream an angel of the Lord reveals to Joseph that the child Mary has "conceived in her is from the Holy Spirit." This marvelous event fulfills the Isaian prophecy that "the virgin shall conceive and bear a son, and they shall name him Emmanuel" (Matt 1:18-24). In Year B, since Mark's gospel contains no infancy narrative, the Lectionary assigns the Lucan version of the annunciation (Luke 1:26-38). The angel Gabriel relays God's message to Mary, that she has found favor with God such that "the Holy Spirit will come upon [her], and the power of the Most High will overshadow [her]; therefore the child to be born will be holy; he will be called Son of God." The Year C gospel passage recounts the sequel to the annunciation, Mary's visit to her kinswoman Elizabeth (Luke 1:39-45). Inspired by the Holy Spirit, the elderly cousin is the first in Luke's gospel to attribute the divine title *Lord* to Mary's yet-to-be-born son. The Holy Spirit plays a central role in all three passages, a sure attestation that God's promises of old are coming to pass. The implied message for subsequent generations of Christians is that if God was faithful to the promises in the birth of Jesus, God will bring all things to fulfillment at the end of time.

With these twelve gospel excerpts the Lectionary expresses the main themes of the season of Advent: commemoration of Jesus' birth and joyful anticipation of his second coming. It is fascinating to note that, through the sequence from the First to the Fourth Sundays, Advent presents time *in reverse*, demonstrating once again liturgy's unconcern for chronological linearity. The First Sunday speaks of the final consummation at the end of time, the Second and Third Sundays narrate incidents related to Jesus' public ministry, the Fourth Sunday recounts episodes announcing Jesus' birth. If Advent is in part a season of preparation for Christmas, the Lectionary implies that Jesus' birth can be understood only in light of the entire mystery of Christ, from his pre-existence to his reigning in glory. Conversely, Advent as anticipation of the second coming makes sense only because of Jesus' first coming. Jesus' entire career, therefore, spans all time and space, embracing the "breadth and length and height and depth" (Ephesians 3:18) of God's passion to save.

Old Testament Readings for Advent

Sunday	Year A	Year B	Year C
First	Isaiah 2:1-5	Isaiah 63:16b-17; 64:1, 3-8	Jeremiah 33:14-16
Second	Isaiah 11:1-10	Isaiah 40:1-5, 9-11	Baruch 5:1-9
Third	Isaiah 35:1-6a, 10	Isaiah 61:1-2a, 10-11	Zephaniah 3:14-18a
Fourth	Isaiah 7:10-14	2 Samuel 7:1-5, 8b-12, 14a, 16	Micah 5:1-4a

Consonant with festal seasons, the Old Testament readings for the Sundays of Advent are selected according to the principle of harmony to express the main themes of the season. With but one exception (2 Samuel 7 read on the Fourth Sunday Year B), all the texts are drawn from prophetic books, and of these, more than half (seven) come from Isaiah. In some of the most resplendent poetry the Hebrew Scriptures have to offer, the prophetic selections rhapsodize about God's imminent intervention to restore Zion and lead the exiled people home. The underlying motifs of abandonment and exile, return and restoration, transformed into the liturgical key of Advent, aptly typify humankind, once burdened with sin and death, now freed by God's mighty act of salvation in Christ Jesus. Three of the passages simply announce the coming of salvation (Isa 2:1-5, First Sunday Year A; Bar 5:1-6, Second Sunday Year B; and Isa 61:1-2a, 10-11, Third Sunday Year B), while in other passages God comes in person to save (Isa 63:16b-17, 19b; 64:2b-7, First Sunday Year B; Isa 40:1-5, 9-11, Second Sunday Year B; Isa 35:1-6a, 10, Third Sunday Year A; Zeph 3:14-18, Third Sunday Year C). The remainder more specifically speak of a messianic figure as the divinely appointed Savior (Jer 33:14-16, First Sunday Year C; Isa 11:1-10, Second Sunday Year A; Isa 7:10-14, Fourth Sunday Year A; 2 Sam 7:1-5, 8b-12, 14a, 16, Fourth Sunday Year B; and Mic 5:1-4a, Fourth Sunday Year C).

On the First Sunday of Advent, the Year A selection from Isaiah paints an idyllic picture of restoration in words that apply even more fittingly to God's end time kingdom than to the ancient time of the Exile: "nations . . . shall beat their swords into ploughshares, and their spears into pruning hooks; nation shall not lift up sword against nation, neither shall they learn war any more." For Year B the Isaiah excerpt voices Israel's heartfelt plea for God to intervene on its behalf: "O that you would tear open the heavens and come down, so that the mountains would quake at your presence." All of this came to pass, for at Jesus' baptism God's voice rent the heavens to proclaim "this is my beloved Son," while at Jesus' death on the cross the earth quaked, releasing its dead. The passage from Jeremiah for Year C prophesies that "in those days and at that time [God] will cause a righteous Branch to spring up for David; and he shall execute justice and righteousness in the land."

The Isaiah 11 pericope for the Second Sunday Year A also presents a Davidic messiah ushering in an idyllic kingdom. From the root of Jesse a branch will grow, and the spirit of the Lord will rest upon him. In the kingdom he will establish, "the wolf shall live with the lamb, the leopard shall lie down with the kid, the calf and the lion and the fatling together, and a little child shall lead them." The Second Sunday Year B offers an instance of correspondence between the first and third readings. The message of comfort which opens Second Isaiah (40:1-10) contains the words cited by the evangelist Mark to identify John the Baptist: "A voice cries out: 'In the wilderness prepare the way of the Lord, make straight in the desert a highway for our God.'" If in Isaiah the people are urged to prepare for God's coming, in the gospel John exhorts the crowds to prepare for the coming of the *Lord*, thus applying to Jesus the title that Jewish tradition used only of God. The same correspondence also graces the selections for the Second Sunday Year C. Baruch's language parallels that of Isaiah when he writes: "For God has ordered that every high mountain and the everlasting hills be made low and the valleys filled up, to make level ground, so that Israel may walk safely in the glory of God." Luke echoes Baruch in citing Isaiah: "Every valley shall be filled, and every mountain and hill be made low, and the crooked shall be made straight, and the rough ways made smooth."

On the Third Sunday Year A, the Lectionary quotes yet another Isaian description of the messianic kingdom. The passage lists the signs confirming its arrival: "Then the eyes of the blind shall be opened, and the ears of the deaf unstopped; then the lame shall leap like a deer, and the tongue of the speechless sing for joy." These are the very signs Jesus accomplishes in his ministry, as related in the gospel selection of the day from Matthew 11, thus creating a strong note of correspondence between the first and third readings. The selection from Isaiah assigned to the Third Sunday Year B enumerates the mighty deeds of God's servant. Proclaimed in the context of Advent, the words apply to Jesus: "The spirit of the Lord is upon me, because the Lord has anointed me; he has sent me to bring good news to the oppressed, to bind up the brokenhearted, to proclaim liberty to the captives, and release to the prisoners; to proclaim the year of the Lord's favor." By citing the words "Rejoice and exult with all your heart" from Zeph 3:14, the Lectionary honors long-standing liturgical tradition of celebrating *Gaudete* Sunday, the Sunday of rejoicing, marking the half-way point to Christmas. The prophet exhorts Israel to rejoice because "the Lord, your God, is in your midst." But there is more. God, too, has cause to rejoice over his people: "He will rejoice over you with gladness, he will renew you in his love. The Lord, your God, will exult over you with loud singing as on a day of festival." Surely this is the same divine joy and delight that, on the night of Jesus' birth in Bethlehem, the shepherds heard "a multitude of the heavenly host" singing.

Because the Fourth Sunday of Advent always falls after December 17, all the biblical passages more directly focus on the upcoming commemoration of Jesus' birth. In close correspondence with the gospels, all three Old Testament readings take the form of obvious messianic prophecies. Thus the Emmanuel prophecy in Isaiah 7, from which Matthew quotes in the gospel passage of the day, appears as the first reading in Year A. In Year B, Nathan's prophecy in 2 Samuel 7 that God will raise up royal offspring from David and will establish his kingdom forever sets the stage for the annunciation story from Luke where the angel reveals to Mary that "the Lord God will give to [her son Jesus] the throne of his ancestor David." Correspondence between Micah 5 and Luke's visitation is less obvious, but the general tenor of the prophecy is not foreign to the events narrated in the gospel: "You, O Bethlehem of Ephrathah, who are one of the little clans of Judea, from you shall come forth for me one who is to rule Israel, whose origin is from of old, from ancient days."

Through the prophetic images of return from exile and of Zion's restoration, the Advent Lectionary adds new shades of meaning to the paschal pattern of God's salvation in Christ: in the coming of Jesus, God has ended humankind's exile under sin; in Christ's return at the end of time, God will restore all things. Moreover, just as surely as God redeemed Israel centuries ago, so also through the work of Christ God's salvation will embrace all people of good will.

Readings from the Apostolic Writings for Advent

Sunday	Year A	Year B	Year C
First	Romans 13:11-14*	1 Corinthians 1:3-9	1 Thessalonians 3:12–4:2
Second	Romans 15:4-9*	2 Peter 3:8-14	Philippians 1:4-6, 8-11
Third	James 5:7-10	1 Thessalonians 5:16-24	Philippians 4:4-7*
Fourth	Romans 1:1-7	Romans 16:25-27	Hebrews 10:5-10
	* readings retained from the *MR* 1570		

In joyfully commemorating the coming of Christ at his birth on the one hand, and devoutly anticipating his return in glory at the end of time on the other, the faithful now find themselves between the two events. These twelve New Testament passages from the apostolic writings, true to their role as second readings, help Christians interpret the meaning of the mystery of Christ and provide guidelines for how they are to behave in the interim—all, of course, as refracted through the prism of the main themes of the Advent season.

The second readings for the Sundays of Advent can be grouped according to the two major divisions of Advent. On the first three Sundays (from the beginning through to December 16) the passages emphasize the theme of eschatology, while on the Fourth Sunday (between December 17 and 24) the excerpts stress the incarnation. Phrases such as "the day of our Lord Jesus Christ" (First Sunday Year B), "the coming of our Lord Jesus with all his saints" (First Sunday Year C), "the coming of the day of God" (Second Sunday Year B), "the day of Christ Jesus" (Second Sunday Year C), "for the coming of the Lord is near" (Third Sunday Year A), "at the coming of our Lord Jesus Christ" (Third Sunday Year B), "the Lord is near" (Third Sunday Year C), echo like a refrain through the first three Sundays.

The readings for the Fourth Sunday turn to Jesus' coming at his birth. In the greeting from his Letter to the Romans read in Year A, Paul describes Jesus as God's Son "who was descended from David according to the flesh," creating a link with the gospel passage of the day where the angel calls Joseph "son of David." In the selection for Year B, drawn from the end of the same letter, Paul writes of the coming of Jesus as "the revelation of the mystery that was kept secret for long ages but is now disclosed," completing the correspondence between the revelation of Nathan's prophecy to David in the first reading and the angel's revelation to Mary in the gospel. The use of Heb 10:5-10 in Year C is less explicitly related to the first and third readings, but the words attributed to Christ, ". . . a body you [God] have prepared for me . . . I come to do your will" (10:5b, 7a) are a felicitous evocation of the mystery of the incarnation about to be celebrated.

The passages for the first three Sundays of Advent exhort the faithful how to behave in the interim, offering a veritable litany of Christian attitudes and virtues:

- "let us live honorably as in the day, not in revelling and drunkenness, not in debauchery and licentiousness, not in quarrelling and jealousy . . ." (First Sunday Year A);
- "we ask and urge you in the Lord Jesus that, as you learned from us how you ought to live and to please God, as, in fact, you are doing, you should do so more and more" (First Sunday Year C);
- "may the God of steadfastness and encouragement grant you to live in harmony with one another . . . ; welcome one another,

therefore, just as Christ has welcomed you . . ." (Second Sunday Year A);

- ". . . what sort of persons ought you to be in leading lives of holiness and godliness . . .; . . . strive to be found by him in peace, without spot or blemish . . ." (Second Sunday Year B);
- ". . . that your love may overflow more and more with knowledge and full insight so that in the day of Christ you may be pure and blameless . . ." (Second Sunday Year C);
- "Be patient . . . strengthen your hearts . . . do not grumble against one another . . ." (Third Sunday Year A);
- ". . . rejoice always, pray without ceasing, give thanks in all circumstances . . . do not quench the Spirit, do not despise the words of the prophets, but test everything; hold fast to what is good; abstain from every form of evil . . ." (Third Sunday Year B, *Gaudete* Sunday);
- "Rejoice in the Lord always; again I will say, Rejoice . . . . Do not worry about anything, but in everything let your request be made known to God . . ." (Third Sunday Year C, *Gaudete* Sunday).

The second readings from the apostolic writings, then, apply the mystery revealed long ago to the daily lives of the faithful. They make it clear that the time between the Lord's first and second comings is not an empty time. It is, rather, a time of grace when the paschal mystery is at work transforming the world, leaving its imprint everywhere so that it might one day reach its fulfillment when Christ comes again. Thus, as they ardently look for the day, Christians are not to remain passive; instead they are to hasten its coming, preparing the way by prayer and deeds of goodness and righteousness. During this time of anticipation, Paul urges believers, both then and now, "to put on the Lord Jesus Christ" (Rom 13:14, First Sunday of Advent Year A) and to "work out your salvation with fear and trembling" (Phil 2:12), resting assured that "[God]who began a good work among you will bring it to completion by the day of Jesus Christ" (Phil 1:6, Second Sunday of Advent Year C).

Conclusion

Advent prepares for Christmas by setting out the larger context of salvation history in which the incarnational aspect of the mystery of Christ can best be celebrated and interpreted. As a season "when that remembrance directs the mind and heart to await Christ's Second Coming at the end of time" (*ILM*, no. 39), Advent sketches the full dimensions of the mystery of Christ and of the salvation he brings, from the Old Testament prophecies to the fullness of the kingdom, thus establishing the context in which the faithful can understand and live out their lives. It is a season that paradoxically exhorts to patience and sobriety all the while stoking the desire for the glorious consummation of all things. In the name of all creation, Christians repeat the ancient prayer of holy impatience, "*Maranatha*! Our Lord, Come!"

9   The Sundays in Ordinary Time

The liturgical year is divided into two kinds of seasons, festal seasons (Advent, Christmas, Lent, and Easter), and Ordinary Time. The difference between the two stems from the way in which the Sundays in each category relate to the paschal mystery. While each Sunday celebrates the entire paschal mystery, the Sundays in the festal seasons stress a particular aspect of it. Advent, for example, waits in joyful hope for the coming of Christ, Eastertide glories in the resurrection. The Sundays in Ordinary Time, however, do not have such an added emphasis. According to the *General Norms for the Liturgical Year and the Calendar,*

> Apart from those seasons having their own distinctive character [Easter, Lent, Christmas, and Advent], thirty-three or thirty-four weeks remain in the yearly cycle that do not celebrate a specific aspect of the mystery of Christ. Rather, especially on the Sundays, they are devoted to the mystery of Christ in all its aspects. This period is known as Ordinary Time (no. 43).

While the Sundays in Ordinary Time may lack a distinctive character, they have the advantage of highlighting the fundamental meaning of Sunday as the original Christian feast. According to I. H. Dalmais, "[t]he thirty-four Sundays *per annum* or of Ordinary Time represent the ideal Christian Sunday, without any further specification. That is, each of them is the Lord's Day in its pure state as presented to us in the Church's tradition."[1] The Sundays in Ordinary Time, then, embody the most ancient tradition. They are Sundays celebrated very much the way each and every Sunday was celebrated in the earliest decades of the Church before solemnities of the Lord and festal seasons developed.

---

[1] I. H. Dalmais, "Time in the Liturgy," *The Church at Prayer: An Introduction to the Liturgy. Vol. IV: The Liturgy and Time,* ed. Aimé Georges Martimort, trans. Matthew J. O'Connell (Collegeville: The Liturgical Press, 1986) 23–4.

During the cycle of one liturgical year, the Sundays in Ordinary Time are organized in a numerical sequence of thirty-three or thirty-four Sundays. The sequence, which is divided into two parts by the season of Lent-Easter, begins at the end of the Christmas season and continues until the start of Lent, and then resumes after the Easter season to continue until the following Advent.

Principles of Reading Selection and Distribution

The Sunday Lectionary reflects the liturgical calendar by employing different combinations of the principles of reading selection and distribution for the two types of seasons. Paragraph 68 of the 1981 Introduction to the *Lectionary for Mass* delineates the characteristics of Ordinary Time in contrast with the festal seasons:

> The decision was made not to extend to Sundays [in Ordinary Time] the arrangement suited to the liturgical seasons mentioned [the four festal seasons], that is, not to have an organic harmony of themes designed to aid homiletic instruction. Such an arrangement would be in conflict with the genuine conception of liturgical celebration. The liturgy is always the celebration of the mystery of Christ and makes use of the word of God on the basis of its own tradition, guided not by merely logical or extrinsic concerns but by the desire to proclaim the Gospel and to lead those who believe to the fullness of truth.

For the Sundays in the festal seasons, the "organic harmony of themes" is achieved mainly through the judicious use of the principles of harmony and of thematic groupings. In some instances, semicontinuous reading also structures the patterns of biblical selections of a festal season, such as for 1 Peter and 1 John during the Sundays of Easter. Finally, more often than not, there is correspondence between two or among all three biblical passages assigned to a Sunday or solemnity. Given the nature of Ordinary Time as a period when the mystery of Christ in all its aspects is celebrated, the Lectionary employs *semicontinuous reading* and *correspondence* as primary, distinctive principles of reading selection and distribution during these Sundays.

Semicontinuous Reading: A modern adaptation of *lectio continua*, the earliest attested reading pattern in Christian history, semicontinuous reading is a sequential reading of a particular biblical book, all the while skipping certain verses or passages. During the Sundays in Ordinary Time, two of the three readings, the passages from the apostolic letters and the gospel excerpts (the second and third readings), are distributed according to this principle: "Beginning with the Third Sunday, there is a semicontinuous reading of the Synoptic Gospels . . . there is a semicontinuous reading of the Letters of Paul and James" (*ILM*, nos. 105 and 107). As a result, the gospel readings and the readings from the apostolic letters each follow their own tracks, with no attempt at linking them according to the principle of correspondence.

Correspondence: Unlike the second and third readings, the first readings from the Old Testament are for the most part selected and assigned according to the principle of correspondence. But even in the application of this principle, the Lectionary distinguishes between the festal seasons and Ordinary Time. For the Sundays and solemnities of Advent, Christmas, Lent, and Eastertide, correspondence, which can link two or all three readings, appears as the last of four principles of reading distribution (in descending order of importance: harmony, thematic groupings, semicontinuous reading, and correspondence). In Ordinary Time, however, correspondence, linking the first and third readings only, is a primary, distinctive feature.

Gospel Readings for the Sundays in Ordinary Time

Sunday	Year A	Year B	Year C
Second	John 1:29-34	John 1:35-42	John 2:1-12
Third	Matthew 4:12-23	Mark 1:14-20	Luke1:1-4; 4:14-21
Fourth	5:1-12a	1:21-28	4:21-30
Fifth	5:13-16	1:29-39	5:1-11
Sixth	5:17-37	1:40-45	6:17, 20-26
Seventh	5:38-48	2:1-12	6:27-38
Eighth	6:24-34	2:18-22	6:39-45
Ninth	7:21-27	2:23–3:6	7:1-10
Tenth	9:9-13	3:20-35	7:11-17
Eleventh	9:36–10:8	4:26-34	7:36–8:3
Twelfth	10:26-33	4:35-41	9:18-24
Thirteenth	10:37-42	5:21-43	9:51-62
Fourteenth	11:25-30	6:1-6	10:1-12, 17-20
Fifteenth	13:1-23	6:7-13	10:25-37
Sixteenth	13:24-43	6:30-34	10:38-42
Seventeenth	13:44-52	John 6:1-15	11:1-13
Eighteenth	14:13-21	6:24-35	12:13-21
Nineteenth	14:22-33	6:41-51	12:32-48

Twentieth	15:21-28	6:51-58	12:49-53
Twenty-first	16:13-20	6:60-69	13:22-30
Twenty-second	16:21-27	Mark 7:1-8,14-15, 21-23	14:1, 7-14
Twenty-third	18:15-20	7:30-37	14:25-33
Twenty-fourth	18:21-35	8:27-35	15:1-32
Twenty-fifth	20:1-16	9:30-37	16:1-13
Twenty-sixth	21:28-32	9:38-43, 45, 47-48	16:19-31
Twenty-seventh	21:33-43	10:2-16	17:5-10
Twenty-eighth	22:1-14	10:17-30	17:11-19
Twenty-ninth	22:15-21	10:35-45	18:1-8
Thirtieth	22:34-40	10:46b-52	18:9-14
Thirty-first	23:1-12	12:28b-34	19:1-10
Thirty-second	25:1-13	12:38-44	20:27-38
Thirty-third	24:36; 25: 14-30	13:24-32	21:5-19
Christ the King (Thirty-fourth)	25:31-46	John 18:33b-37	23:35-43

It is in the selection and distribution of the gospel passages for the Sundays in Ordinary Time that the hallmark of the revised Sunday Lectionary—the assigning of Matthew to Year A, Mark to Year B, and Luke to Year C—is most conspicuous. Except for the Second Sunday, the Seventeenth to the Twenty-first Sundays Year B, and the Feast of Christ the King on the Thirty-fourth Sunday, the Lectionary rigorously respects the fundamental pattern. The feast of the Baptism of the Lord, which closes the Christmas season, is also counted as the First Sunday in Ordinary Time. Janus-like, it serves as a hinge between the two seasons. Because of its historical connection with epiphanic themes, it is usually discussed as part of the Christmas season (see chapter 7 above). The Second Sunday in Ordinary Time exhibits the last vestiges of Christmas-Epiphany themes: "On the Second Sunday of [sic] Ordinary Time the gospel continues to center on the manifestation of the Lord, which Epiphany celebrates through the traditional passage about the wedding feast at Cana [Year C] and two other passages from John" (*ILM*, no. 105).

This semicontinuous reading of Matthew, Mark, and Luke during the Sundays in Ordinary Time covers only part of the story of Jesus. Since the infancy narratives are reserved for the Advent-Christmas season, and the passion, death, and resurrection appear in Holy Week and in the Easter season, only the public ministry of Jesus from his baptism at the Jordan to the eve of his arrest constitute the material for the Sundays in Ordinary Time (Matthew 3–25 in Year A, Mark 1–13 in Year B, and Luke 3–21 in Year C).

Given the 10.5-verse average length of the gospel reading in the revised Lectionary, even thirty-three or thirty-four Sundays cannot provide enough space to contain all of the episodes of Jesus' public ministry as recounted in the synoptic gospels. The compilers of the Sunday Lectionary, therefore, had to be selective. What guided the members of the committee in their selection and distribution process? Three overriding concerns influenced their work. They sought (1) to include as much of the story of Jesus' public ministry as possible, and (2) to underline the uniqueness of each gospel writer's way of telling the story, all the while tailoring the results so as (3) to respect liturgy's need to tell the same fundamental story each year.

(1) In order to incorporate the greatest amount of gospel material within the liturgical constraints of the Sundays in Ordinary Time, a constraint further cramped by the average 10.5-verse limit per Sunday, the designers of the Lectionary turned to modern biblical research for assistance. In the specific instance of the public ministry of Jesus as recorded in the first three gospels, the Two-Document Hypothesis provided the necessary framework for an informed selection of passages.[2] This hypothesis maintains that Mark is the earliest of the three synoptic gospels (Matthew, Mark, and Luke). In writing their gospels Matthew and Luke copied and adapted Mark, Matthew to the tune of 95 percent of Mark, Luke 60 percent. As a result, in a great number of instances all three gospels contain the same episodes. Scholars name the material that is parallel in all three synoptic gospels the Triple Tradition.

Matthew and Luke, however, are nearly twice as long as Mark. Triple Tradition material accounts for only half of their content. Where does the rest of the material contained in these two gospels come from? The gospel material in the remaining halves of Matthew and Luke comes from three sources, each identified by a letter: "Q," "M," and "L." "Q" (from the German word *Quelle* meaning source?) is a putative documentary source containing mostly sayings of Jesus. Although no one has ever seen "Q,"

[2]For a more detailed discussion of the material in this section, see my article "The Synoptic Gospels in the Sunday Lectionary: Ordinary Time," *Questions Liturgiques / Studies in Liturgy* 75 (1994) 154–69.

scholars reconstruct it from material that Matthew and Luke have in common, but which did not come from Mark. Also called the Double Tradition, it represents approximately 25 percent of Matthew and Luke. In composing their gospels, then, Matthew and Luke had access to two documentary sources, Mark and "Q" (hence the moniker Two-Document Hypothesis). Together the material from these two sources accounts for 75 percent of Matthew and Luke. What about the remaining 25 percent? The remaining 25 percent of material in Matthew, which has no parallel in either Mark or Luke, is tagged "M," while the remaining 25 percent of material in Luke, which has no parallel in either Mark or Matthew, is named "L." Scholars are divided over whether "M" and "L" were written or oral sources. In any event, the Two-Document Hypothesis proposes four sources to account for all of the material contained in the first three gospels: Mark, the source of the Triple Tradition; "Q," the source of the Double Tradition; "M," the source of material unique to Matthew; and "L," the source of material unique to Luke.

The identification of the four sources according to the Two-Document Hypothesis underlies the selection of gospel passages for the Sundays in Ordinary Time. For example, instead of repeating Triple Tradition stories in all three years, the Lectionary assigns the bulk of this material in Year B, since it originates from Mark in the first place. This strategy leaves the majority of Sundays in Years A and C free to draw material from the Double Tradition or "Q," a source common to Matthew and Luke, as well as material from "M" (unique to Matthew) and material from "L" (unique to Luke). In the current Lectionary, Year A and Year C in Ordinary Time each contain about an equal number of Sundays presenting "Q" material, with the remaining Sundays in Year A reserved for "M" material and the remaining Sundays in Year C for "L" material. The following table shows the relative distribution of the four different gospel sources in numbers of Sundays:[3]

---

[3]The total number of Sundays in any one Year can exceed thirty-four due to overlaps: in a number of instances, a Sunday pericope includes material from more than one source. In addition, some Triple Tradition material appears in all three years. The complete tabulation would also include the number of Sundays with Matthew-Mark parallels (Matthew copied from Mark, but Luke did not): three in Year A and four in Year B; the number of Sundays with Luke-Mark parallels (Luke copied from Mark, but Matthew did not): two in Year B and none in Year C.

	Year A	Year B	Year C
Triple Tradition	13	23	7
"Q" (Double Tradition)	11		9
"M" (unique to Matthew)	10		
"L" (unique to Luke)			21

By selecting gospel episodes of the public ministry of Jesus according to the Two-Document Hypothesis, the members of *Coetus XI* succeeded in assigning an average of 70 percent of each of the four sources of gospel material about Jesus' public ministry. As a result, almost three-fourths of all the episodes of Jesus' public ministry appear over the three-year cycle of Sundays in Ordinary Time.

(2) In addition to carefully selecting and distributing the material drawn from the synoptic gospels according to the sources out of which they were composed, the designers of the Lectionary also aimed at high-lighting the "teaching proper to each of these Gospels" (*ILM*, no. 105). The Lectionary's selection and distribution of gospel passages for the Sundays in Ordinary Time accentuate the uniqueness of each synoptic gospel in the following ways:

Matthew. Matthew structures his account of the public ministry of Jesus in alternating blocks of narrative and discourse. Five discourses (the Sermon on the Mount, chapters 5–7; the Mission Discourse, chapter 10; the Parable Discourse, chapter 13; the Sermon on the Church, chapter 18; and the Discourse on the Last Things, chapters 23–25) stand out clearly against the narrative background. Most of the material in the discourses comes from "Q" and "M," which contain sayings and stories that, according to the Two-Document Hypothesis, Matthew would have added to Mark. The designers of the Lectionary clearly made an effort to feature this non-Marcan material by selecting excerpts from the discourses for at least half (seventeen of thirty-four) Sundays in Ordinary Time Year A.

Even the narrative sections of the gospel contain teaching material, however. For example, in chapters 20–22, the last narrative section before the passion, Matthew presents Jesus preaching four major parables (the Laborers in the Vineyard, the Two Sons, the Wicked Tenants, the Marriage Feast, read on Sundays 25 to 28). This raises the total of Sundays containing teaching material to twenty-one. Moreover, further to underscore

Matthew's unique contribution to the New Testament profile of Jesus, fully ten of these twenty-one Sundays contain material from "M," gospel episodes found only in Matthew. Among these are such passages as Jesus' saying about comfort to the heavy-laden, his instructions on reproving one's brothers and sisters and on reconciliation, his parables of the Unmerciful Servant, the Ten Maidens, and the Sheep and the Goats. The selections for the Sundays in Ordinary Time Year A, therefore, give prominence to Matthew's emphasis on Jesus as teacher.

As a reading distribution pattern, semicontinuous reading helps capture Matthew's compositional style by maintaining the gospel's original sequence of episodes. For example, the material excerpted from the Sermon on the Mount, the first of Jesus' five discourses, appears in seven successive Sundays, from the Fourth to the Ninth, thus assuring that this important collection of Jesus' teaching is heard in order and interpreted within its gospel context. Narrative segments also gain from semicontinuous reading. For example, to Peter's confession at Caesarea-Philippi that Jesus is the Messiah, the Son of God, Matthew adds the Lord's response, "You are Peter, and on this rock I will build my church." But the episode does not end there. It continues with the harsh debate between the Lord and Peter over the meaning of Jesus' further revelation that "he must go to Jerusalem and undergo great suffering . . . and be killed, and on the third day be raised." The Lectionary divides the incident into two parts, assigning them to two successive Sundays (the Twenty-first and Twenty-second) so as to maintain the flow of Matthew's composition. In another instance, Matthew evokes the Exodus imagery of manna from heaven and crossing of the Red Sea in the tandem stories of Jesus feeding of the five thousand followed by Jesus walking on the sea. Here again the Lectionary maintains the link between the two episodes by placing them on successive Sundays, the first on the Eighteenth, the second on the Nineteenth. Over the course of the long sequence of the Sundays in Ordinary Time Year A, therefore, worshipping assemblies are provided with ample material to get a good taste of Matthew's gospel portrait of Jesus.

Mark. Unlike Matthew, Mark does not divide his gospel into obvious patterns. Some scholars discern a geographical arrangement of episodes: from 1:16 to 9:49 Jesus ministers in and around Galilee; in chapter 10 Jesus and his disciples journey to Jerusalem; from the triumphal entry in chapter 11 through to the end of the gospel Jesus completes his mission in Jerusalem. Other scholars divide the second gospel according to the content of Jesus' ministry: from 1:16 to 8:26, Jesus preaches to the crowds, heals the sick, and exorcizes demons; from 8:27 until the passion narrative (beginning at chapter 14), Jesus turns his attention almost exclusively to his disciples, with very little preaching to the crowds and very few healings. A pivotal incident in both the geographical and content-based views is Peter's confession (8:27-33). At this juncture Jesus decides to head south, beginning his fateful journey to the Holy City where he will finally accomplish his Father's will.

Because of the lack of consensus among biblical scholars in discerning the organizing structure of Mark's gospel, the compilers of the Lectionary do not appear to have followed either pattern but rather were content to select passages that portrayed Jesus in all the facets of his ministry. In comparison with the profile of Jesus presented by the selections from Matthew in Year A, the excerpts from Mark for Year B, since they are drawn for the most part from the Triple Tradition, emphasize the deeds of Jesus. The Year B Marcan selections relate nine healing stories (some of them exorcisms), plus Jesus' stilling of the storm. Many of the remaining Sundays present controversy stories in which Jesus debates with his opponents. The Marcan portrait of Jesus which emerges from these selections is that of a man who inaugurates God's kingdom by engaging the powers of sickness, sin, and evil, even to the point of himself becoming victim of these very powers in his crucified death.

From the Seventeenth to the Twenty-first Sunday in Ordinary Time Year B, the semicontinuous reading of Mark is interrupted by a sequence of five excerpts from John 6 on the Bread of Life. Given that only 60 percent of the gospel of Mark is used in the Sunday and Feast Day Lectionary, the reason for turning to John's gospel cannot be that Mark is too short a gospel to provide enough passages to fill out the thirty-four Sundays in Ordinary Time Year B. The anomaly most probably stems from the realization that setting aside John's gospel for Lent and Easter allows no liturgically suitable niche for the important teaching on the Bread of Life. After all, the Lectionary is a *eucharistic* Lectionary; it would be inconceivable that John 6 not be included somewhere in the three-year cycle. Hence, the Lectionary committee decided to interrupt the semicontinuous reading of Mark's gospel precisely at the moment when it is about to narrate the story of the feeding of the five thousand. John's more elaborate version, therefore, replaces Mark's narrative of the feeding.

Luke. Although Luke, like Matthew, uses Mark as his main source, the third evangelist structures the story of Jesus' public ministry in his own unique way. He divides the story into three main sections: the Galilean ministry (3:1–9:50); the journey from Galilee to Jerusalem, often called Luke's Special Section (9:51–18:14); the Judean ministry (18:15–23:40). Since the episodes of the Galilean ministry appear in Year B, the Lectionary frees up a large number of Sundays in Year C for pericopes drawn from "Q" and "L," most of which are compiled in the travel narrative. Here Luke demonstrates his great literary talent. The travel motif not only provides a handy technique for collecting a wide variety of episodes in the life of Jesus but also adds theological depth by patterning Jesus' turning to Jerusalem along the lines of the Exodus—Jesus' journey to Jerusalem takes on the configuration of a passage through death to new life (Luke 9:31). Because of the travel narrative's importance in Luke's version of the story of Jesus, the Lectionary has selected nearly half of the episodes it contains (twenty-seven of fifty-five), distributing them over the span of nineteen successive Sundays, from the Thirteenth to the Thirty-first inclusive.

To provide the highest profile possible of the teaching proper to Luke, the Lectionary manages to assign most of Luke's special material to the Sundays in Ordinary Time Year C. Nineteen of thirty-four contain "L" material, which includes such well-beloved passages as the episode of Martha and Mary, the healing of the ten lepers, the story of Zacchaeus, and the parables of the Good Samaritan, the Prodigal Son, the Rich Man and Lazarus, the Unjust Judge, the Pharisee and the Publican. From these and similar stories Luke paints his distinctive portrait of Jesus as a man of goodness and gentleness, who seeks out the poor and the lowly, who is merciful and full of compassion.

(3) While the two reasons just cited are geared to offer the broadest selection of the episodes in Jesus' public ministry and to underscore as much as possible the unique features of each of the three synoptic gospels, the third reason considers the needs of the liturgical year. Even a three-year cycle of readings must not obscure the fundamental unity of the liturgical year, during which time the Church celebrates the entire mystery of Christ. Despite the kaleidoscopic variety of biblical selections for the festal seasons distributed over three years, the same basic liturgical themes recur annually. This applies to the Sundays in Ordinary Time as well. Through this long season, the Lectionary plots the same overarching sequence of Jesus' ministry in each year of the three-year cycle. In the words of the 1981 Introduction to the *Lectionary for Mass,*

> This distribution also provides a certain coordination between the meaning of each Gospel and the progress of the liturgical year. Thus after Epiphany the readings are on the beginning of the Lord's preach-

ing and they fit in well with Christ's baptism and the first events in
which he manifests himself. The liturgical year leads quite naturally to a
termination in the eschatological theme proper to the last Sundays,
since the chapters of the Synoptics that precede the account of the passion treat this eschatological theme rather extensively (no. 105).

In addition, to provide still greater continuity from one year to the
next during Ordinary Time, the members of *Coetus XI* opted to repeat key
Triple Tradition passages each year. Jesus' baptism, the calling of the first
disciples, Peter's confession at Caesarea-Philippi, and the debate about the
greatest commandment appear each year in their respective versions:
Matthew in Year A, Mark in Year B, and Luke in Year C. In this way the
Lectionary for the Sundays in Ordinary Time maintains a careful balance
of unity and diversity.

The gospel passages for the Sundays in Ordinary Time, like gospel
readings throughout the Sunday Lectionary, set the tone for the season. If
in Advent the faithful yearn for the Lord's coming at the end of time, at
Christmas they marvel at the revelation of the mystery hidden long ago,
in Lent they renew the journey of conversion, at Eastertide they enjoy a
foretaste of the heavenly banquet, during Ordinary Time they walk the
path of discipleship. Sunday after Sunday, the assembly gathers to receive
the Lord's words and to be inspired by his deeds. Week after week they
walk in his footsteps, following him on the path which leads through
death to new life.

Indeed, each episode in the public ministry of Jesus shows the
paschal mystery at work, transforming the many deaths of human existence into the possibility for renewed life. In the healings, Jesus releases the
sick from suffering and isolation that they might fully participate once
again in life's activities. In the exorcisms, the Lord shatters the bonds of
the powers of darkness that people might enjoy the light of freedom. The
teachings and parables challenge the crowds to see reality anew, fashioned
according to the standards of God's kingdom.

All the stories of Jesus' public ministry, therefore, are mini-experi-
ences of the ultimate transforming passage through death to life. Read
within the context of the Sunday eucharistic liturgy, the ritual context that
allows the word of the scripture to become once again the living presence
of Christ, these gospel passages not only point to the paschal-mystery
configuration of all of human life, they effectively realize what they proclaim. "For while we live, we are always being given up to death for Jesus'
sake, so that the life of Jesus may be made visible in our mortal flesh,"

writes Paul to the Christians in Corinth (2 Cor 4:11). Thus little by little, week after week, the worshipping assembly itself is shaped and molded into the likeness of Jesus, dead and risen, and is called to give praise and thanks for God's transforming action at work throughout the world.

Old Testament Readings for the Sundays in Ordinary Time

Sunday	Year A	Year B	Year C
Second	Isaiah 49:3,5-6	1 Samuel 3:3b-10, 19	Isaiah 62:1-5
Third	Isaiah 9:1-4	Jonah 3:1-5, 10	Nehemiah 8:1-4a, 5-6, 8-10
Fourth	Zephaniah 2:3; 3:12-13	Deuteronomy 18:15-20	Jeremiah 1:4-5, 17-19
Fifth	Isaiah 58:6-10	Job 7:1-4, 6-7	Isaiah 6:1-2a, 3-8
Sixth	Sirach 15:15-20	Leviticus 13:1-2, 45-46	Jeremiah 17:5-8
Seventh	Leviticus 19:1-2, 17-18	Isaiah 43:18-19, 20-22, 24c-25	1 Samuel 26:2, 7-9, 12-13, 22-25
Eighth	Isaiah 49:13-15	Hosea 2:14-15, 21-22	Sirach 27:4-7
Ninth	Deuteronomy 10:12-13a; 11:18, 26-28, 32	Deuteronomy 5:12-15	1 Kings 8:41-43
Tenth	Hosea 6:3-6	Genesis 3:9-15	1 Kings 17:8-9, 17-21a, 22-24
Eleventh	Exodus 19:1-6a	Ezekiel 17:22-24	2 Samuel 12:7-10, 13
Twelfth	Jeremiah 20:7,10-13	Job 38:1-4, 8-11	Zechariah 12:10-11
Thirteenth	2 Kings 4:8-12a, 14-17	Wisdom 1:13-15; 2:23-24	1 Kings 19:16b, 19-21
Fourteenth	Zechariah 9:9-10	Ezekiel 2:2-5	Isaiah 66:10-14c
Fifteenth	Isaiah 55:10-11	Amos 7:12-15	Deuteronomy 30:10-14
Sixteenth	Wisdom 12:13, 16-19	Jeremiah 23:1-6	Genesis 18:1-10a
Seventeenth	1 Kings 3:5-12	2 Kings 4:42-44	Genesis 18:20-21, 23-32
Eighteenth	Isaiah 55:1-3	Exodus 16:2-4, 12-15, 31	Qoheleth 1:2; 2:21-23
Nineteenth	1 Kings 19:9a, 11-13a	1 Kings 19:4-8	Wisdom 18:6-9

Twentieth	Isaiah 56:1, 6-7	Proverbs 9:1-6	Jeremiah 38:1-2, 4-6, 8-10
Twenty-first	Isaiah 22:15, 19-23	Joshua 24:1-2a, 15-17, 18b	Isaiah 66:18-21
Twenty-second	Jeremiah 20:7-9	Deuteronomy 4:1-2, 6-8	Sirach 3:17-20, 28-29
Twenty-third	Ezekiel 33:7-9	Isaiah 35:4-7a	Wisdom 9:13-18
Twenty-fourth	Sirach 27:30–28:7	Isaiah 50:5-9a	Exodus 32:7-11, 13-14
Twenty-fifth	Isaiah 55:6-9	Wisdom 2:12, 17-20	Amos 8:4-7
Twenty-sixth	Ezekiel 18:25-28	Numbers 11:16-17, 25-29	Amos 6:1a, 4-7
Twenty-seventh	Isaiah 5:1-7	Genesis 2:7-8, 18-24	Habakkuk 1:2-3; 2:2-4
Twenty-eighth	Isaiah 25:6-10a	Wisdom 7:7-11	2 Kings 5:14-17
Twenty-ninth	Isaiah 45:1, 4-6	Isaiah 53:4, 10-11	Exodus 17:8-13
Thirtieth	Exodus 22:21-27	Jeremiah 31:7-9	Sirach 35:15-17, 20-22
Thirty-first	Malachi 1:14b–2:2b, 8-10	Deuteronomy 6:2-6	Wisdom 11:22–12:2
Thirty-second	Wisdom 6:12-16	1 Kings 17:10-16	2 Maccabees 7:1-2, 9-14
Thirty-third	Proverbs 31:10-13, 16-18, 20, 26, 28-31	Daniel 12:1-3	Malachi 4:1-2
Christ the King (Thirty-fourth)	Exodus 34:11-12, 15-17	Daniel 7:13-14	2 Samuel 5:1-3

The Lectionary offers an almost bewildering array of Old Testament readings for the Sundays in Ordinary Time. The above table lists ninety-nine different passages distributed over the three-year cycle of thirty-three Sundays, from the Second through to the Thirty-fourth Sunday (the First Sunday in Ordinary Time, the Baptism of the Lord, is counted as the last Sunday of the Christmas Season). Of the ninety-nine passages, eighteen are from the Torah (the first five books of the Old Testament, or the Pentateuch), forty-six from the prophets, eighteen from wisdom literature, and seventeen from the historical books. The table on page 154 shows the relative distribution of these four categories according to the Lectionary year.

Unlike the readings from the apostolic writings and the gospel selections, the Old Testament passages for the Sundays in Ordinary Time are

	Torah	Prophets	Wisdom	Historical
Year A	4	21	5	3
Year B	9	13	6	5
Year C	5	12	7	9
Total	18	46	18	17

neither selected nor distributed according to semicontinuous reading. What kind of patterns, then, underlie the choice and assignment of the first readings? The answers are found in the 1981 Introduction to the *Lectionary for Mass*. Regarding the selection of passages, the document explains:

> To the degree possible, the readings were chosen in such a way that they would be short and easy to grasp. But care has been taken to ensure that many Old Testament texts of major significance would be read on Sundays . . . . [T]he treasury of the word of God will be opened up in such a way that nearly all the principal pages of the Old Testament will become familiar to those taking part in the Mass on Sunday (no. 106).

The key concern of the Lectionary's designers was that over a period of three years the Sunday assembly would hear "all the principal passages of the Old Testament." To establish what constitutes the principal passages, they turned both to tradition and to contemporary scholarship. Experts in the study of liturgy and of the Bible surveyed early Christian records and the ancient Hebrew Scriptures, from which they proposed a list of excerpts that have special pertinence in the story of salvation, particularly as this story finds its center in the paschal mystery of Jesus. From this list the members of the Lectionary committee chose the most important passages. Of course, many of these were slotted for the festal seasons. Others, however, found a fitting location in the Sundays in Ordinary Time where they were linked according to correspondence with already-assigned gospel pericopes. Pastoral considerations led the committee to limit the length of Old Testament passages to an average of 5.5 verses, so as to render the selections easy to grasp, and so that the addition of a third reading to the traditional epistle and gospel might not unduly prolong the Liturgy of the Word.

There are still further reasons for linking the first reading with the gospel according to the principle of correspondence. The Introduction to the *Lectionary for Mass* specifies that "these readings have been chosen to correspond to the gospel passages in order to avoid an excessive diversity between the readings of different Masses and above all to bring out the unity between the Old and New Testament" (no. 106).

The members of *Coetus XI* deemed that three unrelated readings, especially when presented as short excerpts from such disparate categories as the Old Testament, the apostolic writings, and the gospels, would be too difficult for the assembly to assimilate. Providing a gospel mooring for each Old Testament reading helps temper the impression of arbitrariness that three distinct tracks, each independent of the other two, might create. On a more pastoral note, the committee realized that the introduction of the Old Testament as a standard feature in the Sunday and Feast Day Lectionary was a major innovation for Catholics who historically had had so little exposure to it. Consequently they felt it might be best to initiate them to this vast body of literature in manageable doses. Finally, above and beyond the reasons just cited, the systematic correspondence between the first and third readings for the Sundays in Ordinary Time further supports the revised Lectionary's aim of underscoring the essential unity of salvation history. The Old Testament selection places the Christ event within its proper salvation-history context; in turn the gospel passage affirms the Old Testament as the record of God's faithfulness and love toward humankind.

The correspondence between the first and third readings can take a variety of forms and the degree of correlation can vary.[4] The most obvious "is one that Scripture itself suggests. This is the case when the teaching and events recounted in texts of the New Testament bear a more or less explicit relationship to the teaching and events of the Old Testament" (no. 67).

A good example occurs on the Third Sunday in Ordinary Time Year A. In the gospel excerpt of the day (Matt 4:12-23), Jesus quotes the passage from Isa 9:1 in which Zebulun and Naphtali are mentioned. The Old Testament reading selected to accompany the gospel of the day is Isa 9:1-4. Other instances of this type of correspondence can be found in 7A, 10A, 27A, 11B, 18B, 26B, 27B, 29B, 31B.

At times both the gospel selection and the Old Testament passage relate a similar event or deed. A good example appears on the Fifth Sunday Year C where the Old Testament call of Isaiah is paired with the New Testament call of Peter. Similar instances appear on 19A, 21A, 2B, 3B, 15B, 17B, 21B, 32B, 3C, 5C, 10C, 16C, 28C.

---

[4]The following information on the Old Testament selections is drawn from Elmar Nübold, *Entstehung und Bewertung der neuen Perikopenordnung des Römischen Ritus für die Messfeier an Sonn- und Festtagen* (Paderborn: Verlag Bonifatius-Druckerei, 1986) 288–93.

In yet other cases, the Old Testament passage complements or supplements an idea or viewpoint expressed in the gospel. For example, on the Eighth Sunday Year A, God's fatherly care in Matt 6:26 is paralleled with God's motherly love in Isa 49:15. Further examples can be found on 33B, 15C, 23C, 24C, 25C.

Elsewhere the Old Testament excerpt provides background for the gospel pericope: on the Ninth Sunday Year B the Sabbath regulations from Deuteronomy 5:12-15 help explain why the Pharisees object to Jesus' Sabbath healing of a man with a withered hand in Mark 3:1-6. In the same sense are the first and third readings for 11A, 27A, 6B, 8B, 16B, 22B.

In a few instances, the Old Testament reading offers a contrasting viewpoint to the gospel. A good example occurs on the Thirteenth Sunday Year C, where Jesus' saying, "No one who puts a hand to the plough and looks back is fit for the kingdom of God" in Luke 9:62, is contrasted with Elijah allowing the apprentice prophet Elisha to return home from ploughing to bid farewell to his father and mother before leaving to follow his mentor (1 Kgs 19:20).

Finally, at times the connection between the first reading and the gospel is somewhat tenuous, for not every Old Testament passage the committee considered important to include in the Sunday and Feast Day Lectionary could be linked to an already-assigned gospel passage. For example, the only connection between Wis 18:6-9 and Luke 12:32-48 on the Nineteenth Sunday Year C seems to be trust that the awaited day of deliverance will come. Yet, the Book of Wisdom says that "the night of deliverance from Egypt was made known beforehand to our ancestors," while in the gospel passage Jesus urges his disciples to be ready, "for the Son of Man is coming at an unexpected hour." Notwithstanding a few instances of ambiguity, the vast majority of Old Testament passages relate admirably to the gospel. Moreover, the wide variety of correlations between the first and third readings for the Sundays in Ordinary Time shows that the unity between the Old and the New Testaments is not univocal but multifaceted.

The Old Testament passages distributed over the three-year cycle of the Sundays in Ordinary Time are at most a representative sample of the riches contained in the scriptures of Israel. Selected and assigned as they are, they fulfill their liturgical task, epitomized in the Easter vigil and realized throughout the Lectionary, of evoking the broad dimensions of the biblical story and of adding depth of significance to the salvation Jesus brings to the world. Through the weekly proclamation of the ancient story, the worshipping assembly know themselves as a people called to holiness and fidelity by their God who is holy and faithful and learn to discern the essential paschal nature of the entire story of God's dealings with humankind. That is why, in the words of the Apostle, ". . . whatever was written in former days was written for our instruction, so that by steadfastness and by the encouragement of the scriptures we might have hope" (Rom 15:4).

Readings from the Apostolic Writings for the Sundays in Ordinary Time

Sunday	Year A	Year B	Year C
Second	1 Corinthians 1:1-3	1 Corinthians 6:13c-15a, 17-20	1 Corinthians 12:4-11
Third	1:10-13,17-18	7:29-31	12:12-30
Fourth	1:26-31	7:17, 32-35	12:31–13:13
Fifth	2:1-5	9:16-19, 22-23	15:1-11
Sixth	2:6-10	10:23–11:1	15:12, 16-20
Seventh	3:16-23	2 Corinthians 1:18-22	15:45-50
Eighth	4:1-5	3:1b-6	15:54-58
Ninth	Romans 1:16-17; 3:20-26, 28	4:6-11	Galatians 1:1-2, 6-10
Tenth	4:18-25	4:13–5:1	1:11-19
Eleventh	5:6-11	5:6-10	2:16, 19-21
Twelfth	5:12-15	5:14-17	3:26-29
Thirteenth	6:3-4, 8-11	8:7, 9, 13-15	5:1, 13-18
Fourteenth	8:9, 11-13	12:7-10	6:14-18
Fifteenth	8:18-23	Ephesians 1:3-14	Colossians 1:15-20
Sixteenth	8:26-27	2:13-18	1:24-28
Seventeenth	8:28-30	4:1-6	2:6-14
Eighteenth	8:35, 37-39	4:17, 20-24	3:1-5, 9-11
Nineteenth	9:1-5	4:30–5:2	Hebrews 11:1-2, 8-19
Twentieth	11:13-15, 29-32	5:15-20	12:1-4
Twenty-first	11:33-36	4:32–5:2 , 21-32	12:5-7, 11-13
Twenty-second	12:1-2	James 1:17-18, 21b-22, 27	12:18-19, 22-24a
Twenty-third	13:8-10	2:1-5	Philemon 9b-10, 12-17

Twenty-fourth	14:7-9	2:14-18	1 Timothy 1:12-17
Twenty-fifth	Philippians 1:20c-24, 27	3:16–4:3	2:1-7
Twenty-sixth	2:1-11	5:1-6	6:11-16
Twenty-seventh	4:6-9	Hebrews 2:9-11	2 Timothy 1:6-8, 13-14
Twenty-eighth	4:10-14, 19-20	4:12-13	2:8-13
Twenty-ninth	1 Thessalonians 1:1-5b	4:14-16	3:14–4:2
Thirtieth	1:5c-10	5:1-6	4:6-8, 16-18
Thirty-first	2:7b-9, 13	7:23-28	2 Thessalonians 1:11-22
Thirty-second	4:13-18	9:24-28	2:16–3:5
Thirty-third	5:1-6	10:11-14, 18	3:7-12
Christ the King (Thirty-fourth)	1 Corinthians 15: 20-26, 28	1:5-8	1:12-20

The second readings for the Sundays in Ordinary Time are drawn from the letters of Paul, the Letter to the Hebrews, and the Letter of James. Like the gospel readings for this season, they are distributed according to semicontinuous reading, a pattern not entirely new in the revised Lectionary. In a broad sense, the Roman Missal of 1570 already presented a substantial semicontinuous reading of Paul's letters between the Sixth and Twenty-fourth Sundays after Pentecost (except the Eighteenth Sunday). The excerpts from the letters were few, but they were in sequence, and the letters themselves were read in the sequence found in the New Testament: three passages from Romans (Sixth to Eighth Sundays after Pentecost), three from 1 Corinthians (Ninth to Eleventh), one from 2 Corinthians (Twelfth), three from Galatians (Thirteenth to Fifteenth), five from Ephesians (Sixteenth-Seventeenth, and Nineteenth-Twentieth), two from Philippians (Twenty-second and Twenty-third), and one from Colossians (Twenty-fourth) (see table at the end of chapter 1 above).

The revised Lectionary clearly follows the same pattern, but does so in a more systematic way and on a more elaborate scale over a three-year cycle. As a rule it assigns its selections from a particular letter to the same Lectionary year. For example, the semicontinuous reading of Romans is in Year A, of Ephesians in Year B, of Galatians in Year C. There are two exceptions, however:

> Because it is quite long and deals with such diverse issues, the First Letter
> to the Corinthians has been spread over the three years of the cycle at

the beginning of Ordinary Time. It also was thought best to divide Hebrews into two parts; the first part in Year B and the second in Year C (*ILM*, no. 107).

Semicontinuous reading implies a choice. Not every verse of every chapter is selected, in great part because of space constraints—there are only ninety-nine slots for passages averaging 5.8 verses in which to provide an adequate sampling of fifteen New Testament letters. A number of omissions are due to excerpts having already been assigned to the festal seasons. In other instances, arguments or sections of arguments were deemed less apropos for inclusion in a *Sunday eucharistic* Lectionary so highly focused on the paschal mystery of Christ. Moreover, consonant with the role of the second reading generally, the Lectionary tends to favor passages exhorting believers to live lives worthy of their calling as Christians. On the other hand, semicontinuous reading has the advantage of maintaining the sequence of longer arguments by distributing segments over successive Sundays. This is the case, for example, for Paul's elaborate teaching on the Holy Spirit in Romans 8. Although divided into bite-size morsels, most of Rom 8:9-39 is proclaimed between the Fourteenth and the Eighteenth Sundays in Ordinary Time Year A. The same occurs for 1 Corinthians 15, the most extensive teaching on resurrection in the New Testament. Except for the omission of a few verses, the entire chapter is read on four successive Sundays (Fifth to Eighth Year C).

Despite these advantages, the semicontinuous reading of Paul, Hebrews, and James makes the second readings for the Sundays in Ordinary Time the least integrated scriptural passages in the entire revised Sunday and Feast Day Lectionary. Whereas in the festal seasons the second readings from the apostolic writings belong to their liturgical context by virtue of the principles of harmony, thematic groupings, and correspondence, this is clearly not the case for the second readings during the Sundays in Ordinary Time. Distributed according to semicontinuous reading, they follow their own independent track across the sequence of Sundays. Sandwiched between the Old Testament and the gospel readings, they interrupt the correspondence that links them. Nevertheless, two considerations recommend the current configuration. The first is the overriding importance, in light of the consistent witness of history of Christian worship, of systematically including these New Testament letters in a Sunday Lectionary.

The second reason is a renewed appreciation of the role of scriptures generally in liturgy, as explained in Paragraph 68 of the 1981 Introduction to the *Lectionary for Mass*, cited at the outset of this chapter and worth re-peating here:

> The decision was made not to extend to Sundays [in Ordinary Time] the arrangement suited to the liturgical seasons mentioned [the four festal seasons], that is, not to have an organic harmony of themes designed to aid homiletic instruction. Such an arrangement would be in conflict with the genuine conception of liturgical celebration. The liturgy is always the celebration of the mystery of Christ and makes use of the word of God on the basis of its own tradition, guided not by merely logical or extrinsic concerns but by the desire to proclaim the Gospel and to lead those who believe to the fulness of truth.

In the final analysis, patterns of readings are secondary to the fundamental *raison d'être* of the liturgy's appropriation of the scripture: the "desire to proclaim the Gospel and to lead those who believe to the fulness of truth." Both of these goals are achieved in the second readings from Paul, Hebrews, and James for the Sundays in Ordinary Time. According to the paradigm for the liturgical use of scripture determined by the Easter vigil, second readings interpret the mystery of Christ, especially the paschal mystery of his death and resurrection, encouraging the worshipping assembly to discover how their lives, and all of reality, take on the pattern of Christ. The second readings also exhort believers to "put on the mind of Christ," to behave according to his Spirit, transforming their daily lives and the world into the fullness of his risen glory.

Conclusion

Ordinary Time is ordinary only in contradistinction from the heightened time of the festal seasons. Far from ordinary, it embodies the liturgy's oldest, most basic stratum—Christians have been celebrating the paschal mystery of Christ by proclaiming the Word of God and sharing in the Eucharist Sunday after Sunday after Sunday in an unbroken tradition that stretches across the centuries from the earliest decades of the Church until today. More than any other season of the liturgical year, Ordinary Time continues to offer an experience of liturgy's pristine grace and simplicity. The scripture passages assigned on these Sundays, especially through the means of semicontinuous reading and correspondence, preserve the flavor of these ancient times. Proclaimed in such a context, these readings help believers discover that the paschal mystery of Jesus permeates and transforms even the ordinariness of everyday life.

Note on the Solemnities of the Lord during Ordinary Time

After explaining that Sunday "must be ranked as the first holy day of all" (no. 4), the *GNLYC* adds the following specification: "Because of its special importance, the Sunday celebration gives way only to solemnities or feasts of the Lord" (no. 5). While this rule remains in force during the Sundays in the seasons of Advent, Lent, and Easter, both the seasons of Christmas and of Ordinary Time include the following exceptions:

a) Sunday within the octave of Christmas is the feast of the Holy Family;

b) Sunday following 6 January is the feast of the Baptism of the Lord;

c) Sunday after Pentecost is the solemnity of the Holy Trinity;

d) The last Sunday in Ordinary Time is the solemnity of Christ the King (no. 6).

The list of exceptions is further extended where the feasts of the Epiphany, Ascension, and the Body and Blood of Christ (Corpus Christi) are not ob- served as holy days of obligation but instead are assigned to a Sunday. Thus,

a) Epiphany, to the Sunday falling between 2 January and 8 January;

b) Ascension, to the Seventh Sunday of Easter;

c) The solemnity of Corpus Christi, to the Sunday after Trinity Sunday (no. 7).

Finally, although celebrated on the third Friday after Pentecost and not on Sunday, the feast of the Sacred Heart is also included among the solemni- ties of the Lord occurring during Ordinary Time. Since the feasts of the Holy Family, of the Baptism of the Lord, of Epiphany, and of Ascension have been dealt with in preceding chapters, only the solemnities that fall during Ordinary Time need a brief comment here.[5]

The feasts of the Holy Trinity, of the Body and Blood of Christ, of the Sacred Heart, and of Christ the King have all been introduced into the cal- endar during the second millennium of the Christian Church. Because

---

[5]For further information on these feasts, see Adolf Adam, *The Liturgical Year: Its History and Its Meaning after the Reform of the Liturgy*, trans. Matthew J. O'Connell (New York: Pueblo, 1981) 166–80.

each stems from and takes on the trappings of the piety of its era, as a group they are usually characterized as devotional, rather than strictly liturgical, feasts. At times they are also dubbed "idea" feasts, for they celebrate a later doctrinal development rather than a biblical event.

Devotion to the Holy Trinity first appears in the seventh and eighth centuries, but it was not until 1334 that Pope John XXII proclaimed a feast for the universal Church. Coming upon the heels of Pentecost, it summarizes the mystery of salvation celebrated in the Lent-Easter cycle. The feast of the Body and Blood of Christ originated in the twelfth century as an expression of the growing devotion to the Blessed Sacrament. First introduced in the Diocese of Liège in 1246, Pope Urban IV promulgated it as a feast for the universal Church in 1264. Also in the twelfth century appear the first indications of devotion to the Sacred Heart. Its appeal continued to spread, especially through the impetus of the visions of Margaret Mary Alacoque in the seventeenth century, until in 1856 Pope Pius IX made it an obligatory feast for the universal Church. The feast of Christ the King is the most recent. Designed to counter the secular forces of the modern age, Pope Pius XI instituted the feast in 1925 and placed it on the last Sunday in October. The Vatican II reform of the calendar reassigned the feast to the Last Sunday in Ordinary Time, where it crowns the eschatological reflections contained in the readings proclaimed at the end of the liturgical year.

The texts for these solemnities are selected according to the principle of harmony in order to express the main themes they celebrate. Moreover, the three readings assigned to each feast correspond closely with one another. In their own ways, these four devotional feasts add yet other facets to the Church's celebration of the mystery of Christ.

Conclusion

I introduced this book by stating that scripture's home is the liturgy. For, especially in the liturgy, the Church honors the scriptures as it honors the body of Christ. Together God's Word and Christ's Body form the one table from which the Church offers the bread of life for the spiritual nourishment of the faithful. The liturgical proclamation of the scriptures breathes life into them; from it are proclaimed the words that become the Word. I trust that the foregoing analysis adequately illustrates how the Sunday and Feast Day Lectionary plays an essential role in the realization of these mysteries in our midst.

The subtitle *Ritual Word, Paschal Shape* is intended to encapsulate the two main themes that permeate this book. The Lectionary is a liturgical book. It is the Bible ritualized. Liturgical principles and pastoral concerns guide the reading selection and distribution. And because the biblical passages compiled in the Sunday and Feast Day Lectionary, one of the Church's several Lectionaries for Mass, are proclaimed within the context of Sunday and Feast Day eucharistic celebrations, they inevitably, like iron filings near a magnet, point to and take on the pattern of the paschal mystery.

As a result, as much as the revised Lectionary aims at providing a richer fare at the table of God's word so that the faithful might become more familiar with the scriptures, the Sunday Lectionary is not primarily intended to be a Bible course. It is, rather, a patterned selection of biblical texts specially designed to serve the liturgy's work of shaping and molding believers into the paschal mystery of Jesus' death and resurrection. This is not to suggest that exegetical considerations have had no influence in the construction of the Lectionary and that catechetical interests have no role to play in its implementation. On the contrary, the preceding chapters have shown that modern biblical scholarship in many instances underlies the Lectionary's design, and that the Lectionary selections often serve as a basis for instruction, as for example the passages for the Sundays

of Lent and Easter for catechumens and neophytes. Yet even here the exegetical and catechetical concerns gravitate around the Lectionary's liturgical aim of transforming the faithful into the likeness of their Lord. The
liturgy informs by forming.

Stressing the liturgical nature of the Lectionary, as I have done
throughout, has many implications. To explore them here would reach
beyond the intended scope of this study. I would like, however, to offer a
few reflections on how what has been described in this book might im-
pinge upon the human actors in the Liturgy of the Word: the worshipping
assembly, and the homilists and lectors who serve the assembly through
the exercise of their ministries.

Given the ritual nature of liturgy's use of scripture in the Lectionary,
homilists who preach "biblically," who deliver homilies informed by exegetical study of the day's texts, do not for all that fully acquit themselves
of their task. Over and beyond exegetical interpretations, homilists need
to be attentive to how the *liturgy* employs the designated biblical passages.
Why are these texts selected and placed here? What liturgical purpose do
they serve? How do they relate to the full array of passages assigned to the
liturgical season in which they are found? How do they articulate, illumi-
nate, point to, flow out of, comment on, etc., the paschal mystery of
Christ? How do they help the assembly appropriate this mystery so that
their lives are transformed more and more into the pattern of Jesus' death
and resurrection? How do they relate to the great act of thanksgiving to
which they move us? The ritual word must take on a paschal shape.

In the divinely-charged context of the liturgy, lectors play an essential role. Through their speaking forth they awaken the voice that lies dor-
mant in the text. They breathe life into the alphabetic signs on the page;
only by being proclaimed can the encoded words of scripture become the
living Word of God. If it is true that "Christ himself is speaking when
scripture is read in church" (*SC*, no. 7), it can therefore be said that lectors
enable the incarnation of the Word in the midst of the liturgical assembly.
Consequently, it is incumbent upon lectors to understand what they are
proclaiming, and to perfect the techniques of public reading that they
might proclaim with faith and conviction the good news entrusted to
them.

The efforts of lectors and homilists, however, would reverberate
without effect in the absence of a worshipping assembly. It is not enough
for the Word to be proclaimed; it must be attended, pondered, assimi-
lated, celebrated. It fulfills that for which it was sent only when it becomes
enfleshed in the lives of those who receive it. It nourishes and transforms

only those who hunger and thirst for it, like Jeremiah of old who "ate" God's words and found them "a joy and the delight of my heart" (Jer 15:16). Thus the assembled people of God also have an essential role to play in the Liturgy of the Word. By their attentiveness to the proclamation as well as by the intensity of their praise and thanksgiving, but moreso by lives of goodness and compassion, of faith and love, they enable the transforming power of the Word to bear fruit.

The Sunday and Feast Day Lectionary is a sign of Christ's presence among us in our liturgical celebrations. There is perhaps no better way to epitomize its liturgical function than to cite the formula the lector speaks at the end of a reading. Simple and now quite routine, it is a formula fraught with numinous power, for it declares what is happening in our midst to be "The Word of the Lord." In the name of all creation we can only respond, "Thanks be to God!"

Bibliography

Adam, Adolf. *The Liturgical Year: Its History and Its Meaning after the Reform of the Liturgy*. Trans. Matthew J. O'Connell. New York: Pueblo, 1981.

Alexander, J. Neil. "Advent, Christmas and Epiphany," *Liturgy* 4/3 (1984) 9–15.

Allen, Horace T., Jr. "*Common Lectionary:* Origins, Assumptions, and Issues," *Studia Liturgica* 21 (1991) 14–31.

_____. "The Ecumenical Import of Lectionary Reform," *Shaping English Liturgy: Studies in Honor of Archbishop Denis Hurley.* Ed. Peter C. Finn and James M. Schellman. Washington, D.C.: The Pastoral Press, 1990, 361–84.

_____. "Lectionaries—Principles and Problems: A Comparative Analysis," *Studia Liturgica* 22 (1992) 68–83.

_____. "Proclaiming the Word of the Lord," *The Reader as Minister.* Ed. Horace T. Allen, Jr. Washington, D.C.: The Liturgical Conference, 1980, 1–6.

_____. "Understanding the Lectionary," *A Handbook for the Lectionary*. Philadelphia: Geneva, 1980, 11–44.

Anderson, Fred B. "Protestant Worship Today," *Theology Today* 43 (1986) 65–67.

Bonneau, Normand. "Fulfilled in Our Hearing: The Dynamism of Scripture in Liturgical Proclamation," *Shaping a Priestly People: A Collection in Honour of Archbishop James Hayes.* Ed. Bernadette Gasslein. Ottawa: Novalis, 1994, 118–33.

_____. *Preparing the Table of the Word.* Ottawa: Novalis/Collegeville: The Liturgical Press, 1997.

_____. "Sharing at the Table of the Word: The Sunday Lectionary," *Ecumenism* 31/122 (June 1996) 21–3.

_____. "The Sunday Lectionary: Underlying Principles and Patterns," *Liturgical Ministry* 5 (1996) 49–58.

_____. "The Synoptic Gospels in the Sunday Lectionary: Ordinary Time," *Questions Liturgiques / Studies in Liturgy* 75 (1994) 154–69.

Bradshaw, Paul F. "The Use of the Bible in Liturgy: Some Historical Perspectives," *Studia Liturgica* 22 (1992) 35–52.

Bugnini, Annibale. *The Reform of the Liturgy 1948–1975.* Trans. Matthew O'Connell. Collegeville: The Liturgical Press, 1990 [1983].

Chauvet, Louis-Marie. "What Makes the Liturgy Biblical?—Texts," *Studia Liturgica* 22 (1992) 121–33.

Ciferni, Andrew D. "Scripture in the Liturgy," *The New Dictionary of Sacramental Worship.* Ed. Peter E. Fink. Wilmington, Del.: Michael Glazier, 1990.

_____. "Typology/Harmony in the New Lectionary," *The Bible Today* 28 (1990) 90–4.

Congregation of Divine Worship. "Circular Letter *Concerning the Preparation and Celebration of the Easter Feasts,*" *Origins* 17/40 (March 17, 1988) 677–87.

Consultation on Common Texts, *Common Lectionary: The Lectionary Proposed by the Consultation on Common Texts.* New York: The Church Hymnal Corp., 1983.

_____. *The Revised Common Lectionary.* Nashville: Abingdon, 1992.

Dalmais, Iréné Henri. "Time in the Liturgy," *The Church at Prayer: An Introduction to the Liturgy.* Vol. IV: *The Liturgy and Time.* Ed. Aimé-Georges Martimort. Trans. Matthew J. O'Connell. Collegeville: The Liturgical Press, 1986, 1–29.

De Clerck, Paul. "'In the beginning was the Word': Presidential Address," *Studia Liturgica* 22 (1992) 1–16.

Detscher, Alan. "The Second Edition of the Lectionary for Mass," *Liturgy 90* 24/4 (May/June 1993) 4–7.

Dieter, Cheryl, and Brian L. Helge. "The Lectionary for Easter," *Liturgy* 3/1 (Winter 1982) 41–5.

Duchesneau, Claude. "Une liturgie qui tire son inspiration de la sainte écriture," *La Maison-Dieu* 166 (1986) 119–29.

Duggan, Robert D. "Coming to Know Jesus Christ: The First Scrutiny," *Catechumenate* 10/4 (1988) 2–10.

_____. "God Towers Over Evil: The Second Scrutiny," *Catechumenate* 11/1 (1989) 2–8.

Ferrone, Rita. "Lazarus, Come Out! The Story and Ritual of the Third Scrutiny," *Catecumenate* 13/7 (1992) 2–9.

Fiorenza, Joseph. "Sunday: The Original Feast Day," *Origins* 17/31 (January 14, 1988) 529–37.

Fitzsimmons, John H. *Guide to the Lectionary.* Essex, England: Mayhew-McCrimmon, 1981.

_____. "The Revised Lectionary: Achievements and Prospects," *Music and Liturgy* 8 (1982) 95–100.

Fontaine, Gaston. "Commentarium ad Ordinem Lectionum Missae," *Notitiae* 5 (1969) 256–82.

Fuller, Reginald H. "Easter Season Scripture Readings," *Worship* 45 (1971) 220–36.

"General Norms for the Liturgical Year and the Calendar," *The Liturgy Documents: A Parish Resource,* 3rd ed. Ed. Elizabeth Hoffman. Chicago: Liturgy Training Publications, 1991, 173–84.

Gray, Donald, ed. *The Word in Season: Essays by Members of the Joint Liturgical Group on the Use of the Bible in Liturgy.* Norwich, England: The Canterbury Press, 1988.

Greenacre, Roger, and Jeremy Haselock. *The Sacrament of Easter.* Leominster, England: Fowler Wright Books, 1989.

Guillaume, Paul-Marie. "The Reason for an Old Testament Lesson," *The New Liturgy: A Comprehensive Introduction.* Ed. Lancelot Sheppard. London: Longman & Todd, 1970, 59–72.

Jensen, Joseph. "The Old Testament in the New Testament and in the Liturgy," *The Bible Today* 28 (1990) 207–12.

_____. "Prediction-Fulfillment in Bible and Liturgy," *Catholic Biblical Quarterly* 50 (1988) 646–62.

Johnson, Maxwell E. "From Three Weeks to Forty Days: Baptismal Preparation and the Origins of Lent," *Studia Liturgica* 20 (1990) 185–200.

Jörns, Klaus-Peter. "Liturgy: Cradle of Scripture?" *Studia Liturgica* 22 (1992) 17–34.

Jounel, Pierre. "La Bible dans la liturgie," *Parole de Dieu et Liturgie.* Lex Orandi, 25; Paris: Cerf, 1958, 17–49.

_____. "Commentaire complet de la Constitution Conciliaire sur la liturgie," *La Maison-Dieu* 77 (1964) 3–224.

Lathrop, Gordon. "A Rebirth of Images: On the Use of the Bible in the Liturgy," *Worship* 58 (1984) 291–304.

_____. "Scripture in the Assembly: The Ancient and Lively Tension," *Liturgy* 2/3 (1982) 21–3.

"Lectionary for Mass: Introduction," *The Liturgy Documents: A Parish Resource,* 3rd ed. Ed. Elizabeth Hoffman. Chicago: Liturgy Training Publications, 1991, 127–64.

Maertens, Thierry. "History and Function of the Three Great Pericopes: The Samaritan Woman, the Man Born Blind, and the Raising of Lazarus," *Concilium* 22 (1967) 51–6.

Martimort, Aimé-Georges. "À propos du nombre des lectures à la messe," *Mirabile laudis canticum: mélanges liturgiques: études historiques, la réforme con-ciliare, portraits de liturgistes.* Roma: Edizione liturgiche, 1991, 125–36.

Nocent, Adrien. "La parole de Dieu et Vatican II," *Liturgia, opera divina e umana: studi sulla riforma liturgica offerti a S. E. Mons. Annibale Bugnini in occasione del suo 70e compleano.* Ed. Pierre Jounel, Reiner Kaczynski, Gottardo Pasqualette. Roma: Edizioni liturgiche, 1982, 133–49.

James Notebaart, "The Paschal Season, the Days of Sunday," *Liturgy* 3/1 (Winter 1982) 9–13.

Nübold, Elmar. *Entstehung und Bewertung der neuen Perikopenordnung des Römischen Ritus für die Messfeier an Sonn- und Festtagen.* Paderborn: Verlag Bonifatius-Druckerei, 1986.

Ordo Lectionum Missae, Editio Typica Altera. Roma: Libraria Editrice Vaticana, 1981.

Perrot, Charles. "The Reading of the Bible in the Ancient Synagogue," *Mikra: Text, Translation, Reading, and Interpretation of the Hebrew Bible in Ancient Judaism and Early Christianity.* Ed. Martin Jan Mulder. Philadelphia: Fortress, 1988, 137–59.

Proctor-Smith, Marjorie. "Lectionaries—Principles and Problems: Alternative Perspectives," *Studia Liturgica* 22 (1992) 84–99.

Ramshaw, Gail. "The First Testament in Christian Lectionaries," *Worship* 64 (1990) 484–510.

Reumann, John. "A History of Lectionaries: From the Synagogue at Nazareth to Post-Vatican II," *Interpretation* 31 (1977) 116–30.

Regan, Patrick. "The Fifty Days and the Fiftieth Day," *Worship* 55 (1981) 194–218.

_____. "The Three Days and the Forty Days," *Worship* 54 (1980) 2–18.

Rousseau, O. "Lecture et présence de l'Apôtre à la liturgie de la messe," *La Maison-Dieu* 62 (1960) 69–78.

Schuller, Eileen. "Some Criteria for the Choice of Scripture Texts in the Roman Lectionary," *Shaping English Liturgy: Studies in Honor of Archbishop Denis Hurley.* Ed. Peter C. Finn and James H. Schelman. Washington, D.C.: The Pastoral Press, 1990, 385–404.

Skudlarek, William. *The Word in Worship: Preaching in a Liturgical Context.* Nashville: Abingdon, 1981.

Sloyan, Gerard. "The Bible as the Book of the Church," *Worship* 60 (1986) 9–21.

_____. "The Hebrew Scriptures Apart from Their Fulfillment in Christ," *Liturgy 90* 21/7 (October 1990) 9–11.

_____. "The Independent Second Readings and the Psalter," *Liturgy 90* 22/1 (January 1991) 8–10, 13.

_____. "The Lectionary as a Context for Interpretation," *Interpretation* 31 (1977) 131–8.

_____. "Richer Fare for God's People?" *Liturgy 90* 21/5 (July 1990) 8–10.

_____. "Some Suggestions for a Biblical Three-Year Lectionary," *Worship* 63 (1989) 521–35.

_____. "A Treasure-House of Images," *Liturgy 90* 21/6 (August–September 1990) 7–9, 15.

Triacca, Achille M. "Bible et Liturgie," *Dictionnaire Encyclopédique de la Liturgie*, vol. 1. (A–L). Ed. Domenica Sartore and Achille M. Triacca. Turnhout, Belgique: Brépols / Montréal: Sciences et culture, 1992, 129–44.

Truijen, Vincent. "Les évangiles dans la liturgie," *Questions liturgiques et paroissiales* 65 (1984) 213–32.

_____. "La lecture de l'Ancien Testament dans la liturgie rénovée," *Questions liturgiques et paroissiales* 68 (1987) 135–56.

_____. "Les lectures du Nouveau Testament dans la liturgie rénovée," *Questions liturgiques et paroissiales* 70 (1986) 239–51.

Van Olst, E. H. *The Bible and Liturgy.* Trans. John Vriend. Grand Rapids, Mich.: Eerdmans, 1991.

Weiser, Francis X. *Handbook of Christian Feasts and Customs. The Year of the Lord in Liturgy and Folklore.* New York: Harcourt, Brace, and Co., 1958 [1952].

West, Fritz. "An Annotated Bibliography on the Three-year Lectionaries: Part I: The Roman Catholic Lectionary," *Studia Liturgica* 23 (1993) 223–44.

_____. "An Annotated Bibliography on the Three-year Lectionaries: Parts II–IV," *Studia Liturgica* 24 (1994) 222–48.

_____. *Scripture and Memory: The Ecumenical Hermeneutic of the Three-Year Lectionaries.* A Pueblo Book. Collegeville: The Liturgical Press, 1997.

Wiéner, Claude. "L'Ancien Testament dans le lectionnaire dominical," *La Maison-Dieu* 166 (1986) 47–60.

_____. "L'Élaboration du Lectionnaire Dominical et la Consultation de 1967," *La Maison-Dieu* 166 (1986) 37–46.

_____. "Genèse et évaluation du lectionnaire dominical," *La Maison-Dieu* 171 (1987) 111–18.

_____. "The Roman Catholic Eucharistic Lectionary," *Studia Liturgica* 21 (1991) 2–13.

Zimmerman, Joyce A. *Liturgy as Living Faith: A Liturgical Spirituality.* Scranton: University of Scranton Press, 1993.

Subject Index

Index of Names

Adam, Adolf, 130 n 2, 161 n 5
Alexander, J. Neil, 129 n 1
Allen, Horace T., Jr., 52 n 17, 53 n 19, 54 n 21
Anderson, Fred B., 54 n 22
Benedict XV, 121
Bernard of Citeaux, 123
Bonneau, Normand, 52 n 15, 63 n 1, 85 n 4, 98 n 1, 145 n 2
Bower, Peter C., 54 n 22
Bugnini, Annibale, 23 n 3
Clement VII, 123
Dalmais, I. H., 141, 141 n 1
Deiss, L., 24
Diekmann, G., 24
Dalmais, I. H., 141
Emminghaus, Johannes H., 13 n 12
Endean, P., 25 n 5
Feder, J., 24
Fitzsimmons, John H., 60 n 2
Fontaine, G. 23
Gaillard, J., 24
Greenacre, Roger, 65 n 2
Gregory the Great, 114
Guillaume, Paul-Marie, 42 n 8
Haselock, Jeremy, 65 n 2
Hippolytus, 11
Hoffman, E., 32 n 1, 59 n 1
Innocent XIII, 124
John XXII, 162
John XXIII, 21, 22, 23
Jörns, Klaus-Peter, 10 n 9
Jounel, Pierre, 3 n 1, 7, 23, 42 n 7, 45 n 11
Jungmann, Joseph A., 13 n 12
Jurgens, W. A. 10 n 8
Justin Martyr, 9–10

Kahlefeld, H., 24
Lanne, E., 24
Leo XIII, 121
Margaret Mary Alacoque, 162
Marot, H., 24
Massi, P., 23
Murray, R., 25 n 5
Nocent, Adrian, 3, 24
Notabaart, James, 85, 85 n 3
Nübold, Elmar, xiii, 21 n 1, 22 n 2, 24 n 4, 48 n 12, 85 n 4, 155 n 4
Oster, H., 24
Paul VI, 29, 60
Perrot, Charles, 6 n 4, 7 n 6
Pius V, 14
Pius IX, 162
Pius X, 124
Pius XI, 162
Pius XII, 18, 65
Regan, Patrick, 79 n 1
Reumann, John, 3, 12 n 11
Roguet, A.-M., 24
Rose, A., 24
Rousseau, O., 44 n 10
Schaefer, Mary, 40 n 6
Schuller, Eileen, 51 n 14
Schürmann, H., 24
Skudlarek, William, 11, 11 n 10, 32 n 2, 37 n 4
Sloyan, Gerard, 117 n 1
Tillmann, K., 24
Urban IV, 162
Vagaggini, C., 23
Watkins, Keith, 54 n 22
Weiser, Francis X., 118 n 2
Wiéner, Claude, 24, 43 n 9

175